Today's Debates

CHURCH AND STATE

Is a True Separation Possible?

Karen Judson and Erin L. McCoy

Cavendish
Square

New York

Published in 2019 by Cavendish Square Publishing, LLC
243 5th Avenue, Suite 136, New York, NY 10016

Library of Congress Cataloging-in-Publication Data

Names: Judson, Karen, 1941- author. | McCoy, Erin L., author.
Title: Church and state : a true separation? / Karen Judson and Erin L. McCoy.
Description: New York : Cavendish Square, 2019. | Series: Today's debates | Includes bibliographical references
and index. | Audience: Grade 7 to 12. Identifiers: LCCN 2018011645 (print) |
LCCN 2018012141 (ebook) | ISBN 9781502643216 (ebook) |
ISBN 9781502643209 (library bound) | ISBN 9781502643193 (pbk.)
Subjects: LCSH: Church and state--United States--Juvenile literature. | Religion and
politics--United States--Juvenile literature. | Religion in the public schools--United States-
-Juvenile literature. | Freedom of religion--United States--Juvenile literature.
Classification: LCC BR516 (ebook) | LCC BR516 .J829 2019 (print) | DDC 322/.10973--dc23
LC record available at https://lccn.loc.gov/2018011645

Editorial Director: David McNamara
Copy Editor: Rebecca Rohan
Associate Art Director: Alan Sliwinski
Production Coordinator: Karol Szymczuk
Photo Research: J8 Media

The photographs in this book are used by permission and through the courtesy of: Cover Ungvar/
Shutterstock.com; p. 4 Eduardo Ramirez Sanchez/Shutterstock.com; p. 10 Ilene MacDonald/Alamy Stock
Photo; p. 12 Ian Dagnall/Alamy Stock Photo; p. 15, 19 North Wind Picture Archives; p. 27 Superstock/
Alamy Stock Photo; p. 29 Library of Congress; p. 31 Douglas Graham/Roll Call/Getty Images; p. 38
Charlie Neibergall/AP Images; p. 42 AFP/Getty Images; p. 45 Hulton-Deutsch Collection/Corbis/Getty
Images; p. 46, 60, 74 Bettmann/Getty Images; p. 50 Ian 2010/Shutterstock.com; p. 56-57 Raul de Molina/
AP Images; p. 66 Joe Raedle/Newsmakers/Getty Images; p. 69 Hulton Archive/Getty Images; p. 73 Alex
Wong/Getty Images; p. 76-77 NY Daily News Archive/Getty Images; p. 80 Greg Smith/Corbis/Getty
Images; p. 85 Frederic J. Brown/AFP/Getty Images; p. 88 Alamy Stock Photo; p. 93 Library of Congress/
Wikimedia Commons/File:Mothers' Crusade for Victory over Communism LCCN2015648093.jpg/
Public Domain; p. 102 "Many Countries Favor Specific Religions, Officially or Unofficially" Courtesy
Pew Research Center, Washington DC (10/3/2017); p. 109 Courtesy U.S. Commission on Internatioal
Religious Freedom (USCIRF); p. 112 Salampix/Abaca/Sipa/AP Images; p. 117 Vladimir Grigorev/Alamy
Stock Photo; p. 120-121 Roger Lemoyne/Liaison/Getty Images; p. 124 Mads Nissen/AP Images.

Printed in the United States of America

CONTENTS

WE HOLD THESE TRUTHS TO BE SELF-
EVIDENT: THAT ALL MEN ARE CREATED
EQUAL, THAT THEY ARE ENDOWED BY THEIR
CREATOR WITH CERTAIN INALIENABLE
RIGHTS, AMONG THESE ARE LIFE, LIBERTY
AND THE PURSUIT OF HAPPINESS, THAT
TO SECURE THESE RIGHTS GOVERNMENTS
ARE INSTITUTED AMONG MEN. WE···
SOLEMNLY PUBLISH AND DECLARE, THAT
THESE COLONIES ARE AND OF RIGHT
OUGHT TO BE FREE AND INDEPENDENT
STATES···AND FOR THE SUPPORT OF THI
DECLARATION, WITH A FIRM RELIANC
ON THE PROTECTION OF DIVIN
PROVIDENCE, WE MUTUALLY
OUR LIVES, OUR FORTUNES AND OI
SACRED HONOUR.

INTRODUCTION

When Trinity Lutheran Church in Columbia, Missouri, applied for a state grant in 2012, they were hoping to use the funds to replace hard surfaces on the church's playground with rubber. The state, however, denied the grant, claiming that the Missouri constitution prohibited them from spending funds, "directly or indirectly, in aid of any church." In response, the church filed a lawsuit claiming that the state had violated the United States Constitution—in particular, the First Amendment and the Equal Protection Clause, which is part of the Fourteenth Amendment. That lawsuit made it all the way to the US Supreme Court in April 2017. The Supreme Court's decision in *Trinity Lutheran v. Comer* opened up a potential "floodgate of legal

Opposite: This inscription on the Jefferson Memorial in Washington, DC, shows passages from the Declaration of Independence, including references to a "creator" and "divine providence."

challenges." As Justice Sonia Sotomayor wrote, "This case is about nothing less than the relationship between religious institutions and the civil government—that is, between church and state." The stakes were high in a debate that has raged since the United States was founded. In the end, the court voted 7–2 in favor of the church. In his decision for the majority, Chief Justice John Roberts wrote that "the exclusion of Trinity Lutheran from a public benefit for which it is otherwise qualified, solely because it is a church, is odious to our Constitution all the same, and cannot stand." Justice Roberts framed Missouri's denial of funds as an act of discrimination.

However, Justice Sotomayor, along with Justice Ruth Bader Ginsberg, argued that the decision threatened to undermine fundamental American values:

The Court today profoundly changes that relationship [between church and state] by holding, for the first time, that the Constitution requires the government to provide public funds directly to a church. Its decision slights both our precedents and our history, and its reasoning weakens this country's longstanding commitment to a separation of church and state beneficial to both.

The Separation in US Policy

The word "church" refers to any religious affiliation or activity, and the word "state" refers to local, state, or federal governments. The phrase "separation of church and state" is not found in the Constitution of the United States of America, but it refers to the practice of keeping religion and government from unduly influencing one another—a principle that the people who authored the Constitution considered vital to the concept of freedom of religion. For example, because of the "religion clauses" written into the First Amendment—the first of ten amendments called the Bill of Rights—the US government cannot harass Americans because of the religion they practice; nor can it declare any religion the "state" religion and demand that citizens worship accordingly, as in centuries past when people could be jailed or otherwise punished for their religious beliefs. Religion is also not allowed to dictate certain political or legal decisions, such as determining that a portion of public tax monies be given to specific religions or requiring that elected officials take a religious oath or practice a certain faith in order to assume office.

In addition to protections for freedom of speech, the press, the right of the people "peaceably to assemble," and the right to petition the government for a redress of grievances, the First Amendment states, "Congress shall make no law respecting an establishment of religion, or prohibiting the free exercise thereof." These two "religion clauses," called the "establishment clause" and the "exercise clause," respectively, have led to many interpretations on both sides of the separation of church and state issue.

Former President George W. Bush frequently expressed his belief in God and invoked God's blessing. For the first time in the nation's history, Bush established a government office to oversee the distribution of government funds to "faith-based initiatives." The executive order establishing the White House Office of Faith-Based and Community Initiatives (OFBCI) stated: "Faith-based and other community organizations are indispensable in meeting the needs of poor Americans and distressed neighborhoods. Government cannot be replaced by such organizations, but it can and should welcome them as partners."

Some restrictions were nonetheless placed on OFBCI-supported faith-based organizations. For instance, they could not use government funds to support religious activities, such as prayer, worship, religious instruction, or sermonizing to promote a religion. Services receiving government financing could not be combined in time or location with religious services. Moreover, faith-based organizations receiving government funds for community assistance could not discriminate on the basis of religion. That is, one religion, such as Christianity, could not be favored over other religions, such as Islam, Buddhism, or Hinduism.

Critics of the OFBCI—such as Americans United for Separation of Church and State (AU), the American Civil Liberties Union (ACLU), and the Freedom from Religion Foundation (FFRF)— pointed out that no department had been tasked with scrutinizing the payment of federal funds to faith-based organizations. They argued that the OFBCI's activities consistently violated the constitutionally mandated separation of church and state.

Unlike many traditional liberals, President Barack Obama called for faith-based programs that could be proven to work, and ways to track whether those faith-based initiatives actually helped people, something that wasn't done during the Bush administration. More importantly, Obama saw effective faith-based initiatives as those that help people "of all faiths or no faith at all."

In 2009, Obama renamed the OFBCI, calling it the White House Office of Faith-Based and Neighborhood Partnerships, adding additional text to Bush's executive order mandating that "Federal Government funds are provided in a manner consistent with fundamental constitutional commitments guaranteeing the equal protection of the laws and the free exercise of religion and prohibiting laws respecting an establishment of religion." In 2010, the White House added additional safeguards to protect the separation of church and state and enhance the program's transparency. Critics, however, continue to argue that the office's work might condone preferential treatment for religious organizations and protect these organizations' ability to discriminate against LGBTQ (lesbian, gay, bisexual, transgender, queer) employees or those whose religion is different from that of the organization.

Defining the Debate

Within the United States, issues around separation of church and state are sometimes contentious. On one side of the debate are those who have interpreted the Constitution to say that religion has no place in government. People who hold this opinion are sometimes called secularists or secular humanists. (The word "secular" is defined as "relating to worldly rather than religious issues.") Secularists believe that the First Amendment prohibits all religious signs, symbols, and activities on government property. They argue that this prohibition extends to any property financed by county, state, and federal governments, such as public schools. People who take this stance generally have no quarrel with others exercising their religious beliefs, but they hold that such activities should not appear to be sponsored by the government.

The arguments for and against keeping government and religion entirely separate often seem to threaten the core beliefs of both sides. For example, some proponents of separation of church and state maintain that the phrase "under God" should be removed from the Pledge of Allegiance and that the phrase "In God We Trust" should not be printed on coins and currency minted by the federal government. In addition, they recommend against any form of school-sponsored prayer in public schools, including at athletic events and commencement exercises, and that student religious organizations should not be allowed to hold

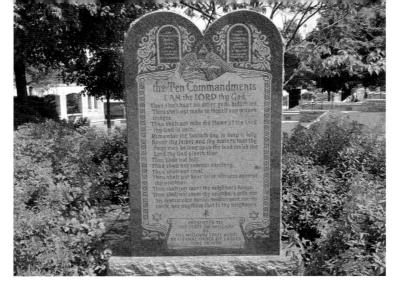

The Ten Commandments from the Abrahamic religious tradition are displayed on the Missouri state capitol grounds in Jefferson City.

meetings in public school buildings. In making these arguments, secularists contend that Christianity is shown a preference when religion intrudes upon matters of state.

On the other side of the separation of church and state debate are those who believe that religion has an important place in government. The rationale for this stance is usually that freely held and freely expressed religious beliefs will enable politicians, officeholders, and others who work within government to make decisions that are more in line with the Christian morals and family values of the general population. The First Amendment was not meant to establish a complete separation of church and state, this side points out, but only to ensure that the government could never designate and fund a state religion. Accordingly, this side argues that prayer, religious displays, and other religious activities should be allowed in public schools and on government property as part of the constitutionally guaranteed freedom to exercise one's religion. If such activities were permitted, however, another question would arise: which religions should be represented, since Americans practice a wide variety of faiths?

People who believe religion has a rightful place in government may also claim that the Declaration of Independence set a precedent (a pattern or a basis in law) for religion in government by using such religious phrases as "endowed by their Creator," "the laws of nature and of nature's God," and "the Supreme Judge of the world." The fact remains, however, that the Declaration of Independence was never a governing document in the way that the US Constitution is.

Despite the strong differences between the two sides of the separation of church and state issue, the debate cannot be explained in simple black-and-white terms. Some people may argue against religious involvement in government affairs but condone prayer in schools. Along the same lines, others may believe that religion has an important role to play in providing moral guidance for individuals as they participate in government affairs, but still be opposed to displaying the Ten Commandments in government buildings.

It is useful to learn about separation of church and state issues because they are often in the news and because individuals who understand all aspects of the argument are better able to make informed decisions when they are called upon to vote for political candidates who take a stance on such issues. Furthermore, since the topic frequently seems to threaten long-held beliefs and opinions, it's important to have an intelligent, considered, and rational discourse to learn what drives the opposite side's argument.

It seems that every president must, at one time or another, take a stance on the debate regarding the separation between church and state. In his first year in office, Donald Trump sought to roll back or weaken the 1954 Johnson Amendment, which bans tax-exempt organizations such as churches from supporting political candidates. In a speech at the National Prayer Breakfast on February 8, 2018, Trump cited the national motto, "In God we trust," as proof that "faith is central to American life." The pendulum continues to swing, and understanding both sides of the debate is just as important today as it was on the day the United States was founded.

Chapter One

FREEDOM OF RELIGION AND THE FOUNDING FATHERS

There is one point upon which both sides of the debate on the separation of church and state can agree: the freedom to practice any religion one chooses is a fundamental American right, as is the freedom to worship as one chooses—so long as doing either does not harm others. Both of these rights date back to the earliest days of American independence, when they were established by two key documents: the US Constitution and the Bill of Rights. It is important to know how and why these documents were drafted in order to better understand the nuances of the church-and-state debate today. Both sides place a high value on the Constitution and the Bill of Rights but interpret them in very different ways.

Opposite: George Washington and other Founding Fathers are depicted at the 1787 Constitutional Convention.

Religion and Early American Colonists

It's an often-repeated fact of history that many of the first settlers who came to America did so seeking freedom of religion, because many of these immigrants—Catholics, Jews, and Protestants of many denominations, including Puritans—had been living under oppressive governments that sponsored state religions and persecuted those who practiced other religions.

However, the colonists themselves were not always tolerant of religious beliefs different from their own. Most agreed that, in matters of social policy, the only correct view was the Christian point of view. Those who did not agree with this were often severely punished. They could be fined, stripped of their personal belongings or land, ostracized, banished, jailed, beaten, tortured—even killed.

For example, Anne Hutchinson migrated with her husband and children from England to the Massachusetts Bay Colony in 1634. Hutchinson, an educated woman for her time, soon organized groups to discuss recent church sermons and her own religious views. People did not need ministers to communicate with God, Hutchinson believed, and God's promise of forgiveness alone could gain a sinner admission to heaven. Magistrates (local government officials) and pastors began to attend Hutchinson's sessions, and they strongly disagreed with many of her beliefs.

Hutchinson was arrested in 1637 and tried in a Massachusetts Bay Colony court for her views. Governor John Winthrop presided over Hutchinson's trial. In his opening remarks, Winthrop said, "Mrs. Hutchinson, you are called here as one of those that have troubled the peace of the commonwealth and the churches here."

Hutchinson had no lawyer to represent her in court, and she faced a panel of forty-nine men who accused her of eighty-two unlawful acts, including sedition (trying to overthrow the

Anne Hutchinson, who stood up for her own religious views in the Massachusetts Bay Colony, is banished from the colony in 1637.

government), voicing opinions that were offensive to God, and overstepping her place as a woman. The panel found Hutchinson guilty and banished her from the colony. She left in the spring of 1638 and eventually found her way to Providence, in Rhode Island Colony.

At about the same time, Roger Williams was also angering the religious-political leaders of the Massachusetts Bay Colony.

Williams, like Hutchinson, was a Puritan who believed that the Church of England was not a true Christian church because it had not been "purified" of worldly ceremonies and institutions. Williams continued to disturb Governor Winthrop and other leaders of the Massachusetts Bay Colony with his admonition that Puritans must expressly separate from the Church of England and his insistence that the land the settlers inhabited should be purchased, rather than simply taken, from the Native Americans who actually owned it. Williams was banished from the colony in 1635, and he fled to the area that in 1636 would become Rhode Island Colony. He founded Providence—on land that he bought from the Native Americans—and he welcomed others who had fled religious persecution.

Incidents of religious persecution would take place throughout the thirteen colonies, which were Connecticut, Delaware, Georgia, Maryland, Massachusetts, New Hampshire, New Jersey, New York, North and South Carolina, Pennsylvania, Virginia, and Rhode Island. In many cases, Quakers were singled out for harsh punishment, primarily because their religion was vastly different from other Protestant faiths. The Quakers, also known as the Society of Friends, held to no specific creed. They had no professional clergy and no sacraments of liturgy, since their faith emphasized the inner relationship of a person with God, rather than outward manifestations of Christianity. The Quaker religion forbade its followers to swear oaths to the government or serve in the military, and for this reason, followers of other religions often suspected Quakers of sedition and cowardice. Some colonies enacted anti-Quaker laws that enabled authorities to banish Quakers. Sometimes the "crime" of being a Quaker was also punishable by whipping, mutilation, or death.

Despite evidence of religious persecution in the New World, immigrants seeking a better life continued to arrive in America.

By 1700, the population in the northeastern United States had reached 250,000, with Boston the most-populous city (7,000) and New York City the second–most populous (5,000). Population increases meant more trade and commerce, which in turn meant establishing governments to levy taxes and enforce regulations. The American colonies were still under British rule, and from 1620 to 1700, British monarchs appointed a series of governors to govern the settlements. Many colonists grew increasingly unhappy with British rule in the 1700s, citing taxation without representation, repressive laws, and other practices designed to further Great Britain's interests while disregarding the welfare of colonial settlers.

Although Britain remained the governing nation, colonial settlements could obtain a charter from Britain allowing them to form their own local governments. The first town government in the colonies was organized in Dorchester, Massachusetts, in 1633. Local governments passed laws pertaining to business activities, the payment of debts, the mandated observance of Sunday as a holy day, and other matters related to the daily lives of settlers. Local governments could also restrict religious freedom at will. Such local laws were allowed to stand as long as they did not conflict with British law.

In 1689, Britain passed the Toleration Act, which mandated toleration of all Protestants who swore an oath of allegiance to the English monarchy and rejected the doctrine of transubstantiation. (Transubstantiation refers to the Roman Catholic and Eastern Orthodox doctrine by which the bread and wine of communion become—in substance, though not appearance—the actual body and blood of Jesus Christ at consecration.) The Toleration Act applied to all the colonies as well as to Britain, which meant that civil and religious societies in the colonies were assumed to be Protestant.

The Great Awakening

During the eighteenth century, many people in Germany, France, Britain, and other European countries practiced a philosophy that valued reason, rationality, and scientific proof over the more otherworldly aspects of religion. This intellectual movement, predominant first in Europe and then in the American colonies, was called the Age of Enlightenment.

As the Age of Enlightenment influenced society both in Europe and in the American colonies, religious fervor declined. Then, during the mid-eighteenth century (approximately 1730–1760), the First Great Awakening swept across Europe and the colonies. This movement ushered in a new age of faith to counter the intellectualizing forces that had gained influence during the Age of Enlightenment. To be truly religious, Great Awakening leaders proclaimed, one must trust the heart rather than the head, prize feeling over thinking, and rely on the Bible's teachings rather than human reason.

The American phase of the Great Awakening began among Presbyterians in Pennsylvania and New Jersey. William Tennent, who arrived in the colonies in 1718, and his four sons, all Scotch-Irish Presbyterian ministers, led revivalist meetings in Pennsylvania, exhorting Christians to repent their sinful ways and spread the word of God. Tennent also established a school for clergy called the Log College, known today as Princeton University.

Jonathan Edwards, a well-educated Congregationalist minister who lived in Northampton, Massachusetts, was also a prominent figure in the Great Awakening. In his famous 1741 sermon, "Sinners in the Hands of an Angry God," delivered in Enfield, Massachusetts, Edwards invoked the image of sinners as spiders, suspended by thin filaments over a fiery hell that he said awaits all those who fail to repent.

George Whitefield, shown in 1742, preached throughout Great Britain and the American colonies during the Great Awakening.

Inspired by evangelical ministers such as Edwards and Tennent, itinerant preachers traveled throughout the colonies preaching their fire-and-brimstone versions of the gospel to congregations at revivalist meetings. Among the ranks of traveling preachers were even a few women and African Americans, and many were moved to serve as missionaries to the Southern colonies.

Critics deplored the emotionalism as hundreds of loud, enthusiastic conversions occurred "from the heart," rather than "from the head." Still, the number of converts continued to increase.

Although the Great Awakening took place over the course of a few decades, it had a lasting impact on American society. Richard L. Bushman, a leading scholar of US religious history, explained the effects of the Great Awakening on colonial America:

[Between just 1740 and 1743] thousands were converted. People from all ranks of society, of all ages, and from every section underwent the new birth. In New England, virtually every congregation was touched. It was not uncommon for ten or twenty percent of a town, having experienced grace, to join the church in a single year ... It is safe to say that most of the colonists in the 1740s, if not converted themselves, knew someone who was, or at least heard revival preaching.

Historians have suggested that the eighteenth century's Great Awakening helped prepare American colonists for the challenges they would face as they sought to separate from Britain's rule. Some of those who converted to a more evangelical version of the Christian faith, for example, challenged their local clergy to become more passionate in preaching the need for salvation and left those congregations that refused to change. Others exhorted local governments to stop financially supporting one faith over others and to repeal laws that penalized followers of certain faiths. In short, this generation of citizens learned the importance of self-determination and even rebellion against the existing ranks of power and privilege—lessons that would serve them well as the colonies moved toward independence.

The Formation of a New Nation

The first shots of the American Revolution were fired in 1775. Fearing that an American rebellion was coming, the British government dispatched soldiers to capture a large cache of weapons in Concord, Massachusetts. Local militiamen defended the weapons depot, and the American Revolution began.

A national congress was quickly assembled to organize the Continental Army, with George Washington serving as commander in chief. The poorly supplied Continental Army fought on while the Continental Congress met to declare independence from Britain. Members introduced a resolution stating that the "United Colonies are, and of right ought to be, free and independent States." A special committee was appointed and asked to "prepare a declaration to the effect of the said first resolution." The result was the Declaration of Independence, which was adopted on July 4, 1776. Thomas Jefferson, who drafted the declaration, wrote that the power of government would thereafter derive from the governed.

The American volunteer army defeated the British to end the American Revolution in 1781. In February 1782, the British House of Commons voted against further military action in the United States. The 1783 Treaty of Paris formally recognized American independence.

When the American Revolution ended, the Articles of Confederation passed by the Continental Congress in 1781 loosely governed the states. Each state had one vote in Congress, but only the individual states could regulate commerce, levy taxes, maintain an army, or print money. The United States was therefore simply a loose-knit group of bickering and competing states. Important legislation seldom passed, because at least nine of the thirteen states had to agree to pass national laws. Meanwhile, the colonies were about $42 million in debt after the war, with no way to legislate payment of the debt.

In January 1787, eleven hundred farmers in Massachusetts, many of them veterans of the American Revolution, took up arms against the state government. The group held off the state militia for five months before the rebels were defeated. Seventeen days after Shays's Rebellion ended, the states agreed to hold a convention to revise the Articles of Confederation, establishing a stronger federal government. The thirteen states were free to send as many delegates as they wanted. Only Rhode Island did not send delegates to the Constitutional Convention. The convention met in Philadelphia, Pennsylvania, in May 1787, and four months later, delegates had written and signed the Constitution of the United States of America.

The Constitution and the Bill of Rights

The men who wrote the Constitution are often called America's Founding Fathers. "Founding Fathers" is an inexact term that refers to the fifty-five delegates to the 1787 Constitutional Convention. (Fifteen of the delegates were unable to stay until the end of the convention, and therefore are not listed as signers of the Constitution.) Others who are often considered Founding Fathers are the fifty-six signers of the Declaration of Independence, the members of the first US Congress in 1789, and the first Supreme Court justices, who served from 1789 to 1795.

The Constitution could not become the law of the land until at least nine of the thirteen states had ratified it. The document was sent to the states for consideration in the fall of 1787, and various groups actively campaigned for and against its ratification. States were to retain all rights and responsibilities not expressly given to the federal government, so the sovereignty of the states had been maintained by the writers of the Constitution. However, critics argued that it conferred too much power on the federal government. Others believed the document should have contained a bill of rights to protect the rights of individuals against an all-powerful authority. Despite arguments against the Constitution, the required number of states voted for ratification, and the Constitution officially became law in March 1789.

Although delegate George Mason of Virginia suggested that a bill of rights be included in the Constitution, other delegates argued that such a bill was not necessary, because the document already protected individual liberties as drafted. For example, Article I, Section 10, of the Constitution prohibited Congress and state legislatures from passing bills of attainder—acts that allowed people to be arrested and punished without a trial—and Article VI said there could be no religious tests as a requirement for public office.

Despite all the arguments maintaining that the Constitution, as written, protected basic rights, the movement in support of a bill of rights grew. Although the required number of states ratified the Constitution, the approval was granted only on the condition that a list of individual liberties, expressly guaranteed by the new government, would be compiled immediately.

Consequently, when the first Congress of the United States met in 1789, one of its first acts was to create the Bill of Rights. US Representative James Madison drafted a list of nineteen rights, compiled from more than two hundred suggestions submitted by the states. By September 25, 1789, the Senate and the House of Representatives had agreed on twelve provisions, and the new Bill of Rights was sent to each of the states for ratification. The states approved ten rights—laid out in amendments—out of the twelve for final ratification, and the Bill of Rights became law in December 1791.

James Madison argued for an amendment that would make the Bill of Rights binding on state governments, as well as on the federal government, but Congress did not act on Madison's suggestion. As a result, for decades afterward, many state laws were passed that violated individual liberties. This mistake was corrected with the Fourteenth Amendment, ratified in 1868, which made the Bill of Rights binding on state governments. The amendment proclaims: "No State shall make or enforce any law which shall abridge the privileges or immunities of citizens of the United States."

The First Amendment

The writers of the US Constitution did not confer any explicit power of the federal government to act in the area of religion because they wanted to ensure that no religion would ever be favored or harassed by the government. The First Amendment, however, was added when the Bill of Rights was written to explicitly guarantee freedom of religion and freedom of worship.

When discussing the First Amendment, individuals sometimes forget that "freedom of religion" also includes the freedom not to be religious. Thomas Jefferson, author of the Declaration of Independence and an influential landowner, businessman, and politician, felt strongly that Americans should be free to practice any religion or no religion at all. He was out of the country when the Constitutional Convention met in Philadelphia in 1787, but evidence that he thought the government should not favor one religion over another, or religion over lack of religion, is found in his book, *Notes on the State of Virginia*: "The legitimate powers of government extend to such acts only as are injurious to others. But it does me no injury to my neighbor to say there are twenty gods or no god. It neither picks my pocket nor breaks my leg."

Clearly, the relationship between religion and government was important to the framers of the Constitution, as evidenced by the full text of the First Amendment:

Religious Freedom in the Constitution

Other guarantees in the Constitution also pertain to religious freedom. For example, Article VI provides that "no religious Test shall ever be required as a Qualification of any Office or public Trust under the United States." In other words, Article VI meant that government employees could not be required to swear to certain religious beliefs as a condition of office or employment. Article II of the Constitution, however, allows (though it does not require) the president to make an "affirmation" of the faithful execution of his duties. The framers of the Constitution suggested appropriate wording for such an affirmation, with no mention of religion, and the following president's Oath of Office, from Article II, Section I, of the US Constitution has been used ever since: "I do solemnly swear (or affirm) that I will faithfully execute the office of President of the United States, and will to the best of my ability, preserve, protect and defend the Constitution of the United States."

Although the Constitution made it clear that the federal government would not require a religious test for its employees, state governments have not always followed suit. The US Constitution proscribed regulations and procedures for the federal government, but each state also had its own constitution that could include a state bill of rights or declaration of rights. Seven states—Texas, Massachusetts, Maryland, North Carolina, Pennsylvania, South Carolina, and Tennessee—required that state office holders believe in a supreme being and in a future state of rewards and punishments. In some of the seven states mentioned above, the oath of office must include the words "so help me God." These religious requirements are still on the books in these states, but the Fourteenth Amendment to the Constitution and subsequent US Supreme Court decisions have rendered them unenforceable.

Congress shall make no law respecting an establishment of religion, or prohibiting the free exercise thereof; or abridging the freedom of speech, or of the press; or the right of the people peaceably to assemble, and to petition the Government for a redress of grievances.

The establishment clause within the First Amendment—"Congress shall make no law respecting an establishment of religion"—was meant to prevent the federal government from designating and financially supporting a national religion. The free exercise clause in the same amendment—"or prohibiting the free exercise thereof"—ensured that people in the United States would be free to pray, attend church services, and otherwise practice their religion as they desired, without national government interference, as long as their religious practices did not infringe on the rights of others. However, the states continued to interfere in religious practices for some time after the First Amendment became law.

Interpreting the First Amendment

Since the First Amendment was written, Americans have been debating how to interpret the religion clauses. Many of those who believe in a broad interpretation of the separation of church and state argue that most of the framers themselves were Christians, and they would certainly have wanted the government to reflect the Christian faith. If the government acts favorably toward Christianity, they argue, that does not mean it is endorsing or establishing a national religion.

Although evidence supports the assertion that the majority of the Founding Fathers were not atheists (people who do not

> CONGRESS SHALL MAKE NO LAW *respecting an establishment of religion, or prohibiting the free exercise thereof; or abridging the freedom of speech, or of the press; or the right of the people peaceably to assemble, and to petition the Government for a redress of grievances.*
>
> ❦ **THE FIRST AMENDMENT TO THE U.S. CONSTITUTION**
> 15 DECEMBER 1791

The First Amendment includes both the establishment clause—
"Congress shall make no law respecting an establishment of religion"—
and the exercise clause—"or prohibiting the free exercise thereof."

believe in God), it may be true that they weren't Christians either. Some historians have claimed that many of the Founding Fathers were deists. That is, they believed in a creator of the universe—a God of nature—who did not concern himself with the affairs of humans and did not communicate with humans. Unlike Christians, deists generally did not believe that the Bible was the written word of God.

Most of the Founding Fathers were students of the Age of Enlightenment, also called the Age of Reason, and so had thoughtfully considered religious beliefs other than the traditional Christian doctrines. Strongly influenced by the rise of modern science and by the aftermath of the long religious conflict that followed the Protestant Reformation in Europe, the thinkers of the Enlightenment, sometimes called philosophes (not philosophers), were committed to secular views based on reason or human understanding only.

Influential men of colonial times were sometimes called upon to explain their religious beliefs, but they seldom did so in the words of mainstream Christianity. For example, in 1790, in correspondence with his friend Ezra Stiles, Founding Father Benjamin Franklin wrote of his own religious beliefs:

Here is my creed. I believe in one God, creator of the universe. That he governs by his providence. That he ought to be worshipped. That the most acceptable service we render to him is doing good to his other children. That the soul of man is immortal, and will be treated with justice in another life respecting its conduct in this … As to Jesus of Nazareth, my opinion of whom you particularly desire, I think the system of morals and his religion, as he left them to us, the best the world ever saw or is likely to see.

George Washington—who served as commander in chief of the Continental Army, presided over the Constitutional Convention, and was the first president of the United States—often used the phrase "under God" when issuing written military orders. He also scheduled religious services for his troops, ordering all soldiers to attend. He seldom referred to religion after he left the military, but according to several biographers, Washington practiced religious tolerance and had expressed pride that the US Constitution granted freedom of religion to all Americans, especially to formerly persecuted groups such as the Jews and Quakers. In a letter to the Quakers, Washington wrote: "The liberty enjoyed by the People of these States, of worshipping Almighty God agreeable to their consciences is not only among the choicest of their blessings but also of their rights … I assure you very explicitly that in my opinion the conscientious scruples of all men should be treated with delicacy and tenderness." Still,

THOMAS JEFFERSON
President of the United States.

Thomas Jefferson, a Founding Father and the third president of the
United States, strongly supported religious liberty.

when he left the presidency in 1797, George Washington said in his farewell address that religion, as a source of morality, was "a necessary spring of popular government."

Although Thomas Jefferson professed a belief in God, he also believed strongly in the protection of religious liberty for all Americans. On New Year's Day, 1802, President Jefferson wrote a letter in which he explained his reasons for refusing to issue presidential proclamations for days of public fasting and thanksgiving. He wrote:

Believing with you that religion is a matter which lies solely between Man & his God, that he owes account to none other for his faith or his worship, that the legitimate powers of government reach actions only, & not opinions, I contemplate with sovereign reverence that act of the whole American people which declared that their legislature should "make no law respecting an establishment of religion, or prohibiting the free exercise thereof," thus building a wall of separation between Church & State.

Jefferson's wall of separation has endured as the metaphor that many believe best symbolizes the Constitution's intent in matters of religion and the state. In *Thomas Jefferson and the Wall of Separation Between Church and State*, Daniel L. Dreisbach points out that the "wall" Jefferson erected in the Danbury letter was between the federal government on one side and church authorities and state government on the other. Only after ratification of the Fourteenth Amendment in 1868 would First Amendment restrictions also be applied to state governments.

The freedom of religion was a core tenet of the Founding Fathers, but even in their time, they were called upon to interpret the idea and how it should be carried out. Politicians throughout US history have sought to do the same, using their own interpretations of the Constitution and the Bill of Rights to support their arguments.

Chapter Two

RELIGION'S PLACE IN POLITICS

Religion has an indisputable effect on US politics
today. In the 2012 and 2016 presidential elections, at least
70 percent of white evangelical Protestants supported the
Republican candidate, while more than 65 percent of religiously
unaffiliated voters opted for the Democratic candidate,
according to the Pew Research Center. Even given this
divide, the number of Americans who preferred a president
with "firm religious convictions" was actually declining
in 2016: 62 percent had this preference, compared to
67 percent in 2012 and 72 percent in 2009. Religion
nonetheless has been and remains closely intertwined
with American politics, even if many secularists believe
this connection endangers the freedom of religion.

Opposite: Father Daniel P. Coughlin, then-chaplain of the US House
of Representatives, delivers an invocation, or prayer, during a joint
meeting of Congress in New York City in 2002.

Religion and Presidents

That religion has always been present in politics is clear from the rhetoric during state and federal election campaigns throughout American history. For example, Thomas Jefferson, whose writing about church and state led voters to doubt his religious beliefs, spent much of his 1800 election campaign disavowing charges that he was an atheist. Timothy Dwight, who was at the time president of Yale University and a Congregationalist minister, warned that if Jefferson became president, "we may see the Bible cast into a bonfire, the vessels of the sacramental supper borne by an ass in public procession, and our children … chanting mockeries against God … [to] the ruin of their religion, and the loss of their souls." Advertisements published during the election said voters could have "[John] Adams and God, or Jefferson and no God." Despite accusations about his religious beliefs, however, Jefferson won the election.

Once elected, US presidents and other elected officials continue to face situations that require them to either reaffirm their own religious convictions or resist pressure to give Christianity more of a voice in government.

For instance, in 1808, Jacob Henry, a Jewish man, won election to North Carolina's state legislature. State requirements for office, however, prevented Henry from being seated unless he became a Protestant and unless he would concede the divine authority of the New Testament. Jews follow the Old Testament and don't believe in the New Testament. Henry risked expulsion from office when he refused to take his oath of office on the New Testament. He delivered a speech, saying, "Governments only concern the actions and conduct of man, and not his speculative notions. Who among us feels himself so exalted above his fellows as to have a right to dictate to them any mode of belief?" Henry was allowed to take his seat in the North Carolina state legislature.

Abraham Lincoln, the country's sixteenth president, did not support a proposal to amend the Preamble to the US Constitution, but neither did Congress nor any of the states. The Preamble, as it was originally written, said: "We the people of the United States, in order to form a more perfect union, establish justice, insure domestic tranquility, provide for the common defense, promote the general welfare, and secure the blessings of liberty to ourselves and our posterity, do ordain and establish this Constitution for the United States of America."

The suggested amendments to the Preamble were (with proposed changes italicized):

We, the people of the United States, humbly acknowledging almighty God as the source of all authority and power in civil government, the Lord Jesus Christ as the ruler among nations, his revealed will as the supreme law of the land, in order to constitute a Christian government, and *in order to form a more perfect union, establish justice, insure domestic tranquility, provide for the common defense, promote the general welfare, and secure* the inalienable rights and *the blessings of* life, liberty, and the pursuit of happiness to ourselves, our posterity, and all the people, *do ordain and establish this Constitution for the United States of America.*

Despite the resistance of such individuals as Henry and Lincoln to the direct association of the Christian religion with the US government, almost all presidents have identified as Christian, and presidents today freely invoke God in public speeches. It has also become common practice for political candidates

Religion and Presidential Elections

History has shown that when candidates run for president, religion frequently enters the debate:

- Andrew Jackson, the nation's seventh president, resisted the political pressure to form a Christian Party in politics.
- William McKinley argued that he was a better Protestant than his 1896 opponent for president, William Jennings Bryan.
- Theodore Roosevelt said that the president should attend church regularly, in order to serve as an example to others.
- In the 1908 presidential election, supporters of candidate William Jennings Bryan, who was an evangelical Christian, attacked his Unitarian opponent, William Howard Taft, calling him "an apostate." (An apostate is one who abandons his faith, cause, or principles.) Taft was elected the nation's twenty-seventh president.
- In the early 1950s, Dwight Eisenhower assured American voters that belief in God was the first principle of Americanism.
- John F. Kennedy, a Catholic, assured voters that if elected president, he would not do the pope's bidding. Kennedy became the first Catholic president of the United States—and remains the only one to date.
- President George W. Bush frequently referred to his faith in public.
- As a candidate, President Barack Obama made it clear that his faith was important to him.

to discuss religion—both their own and their opponents'—during campaigns.

In the campaign for the 2008 presidential election, for example, candidates of both political parties rushed to assure voters of their belief in God and "family values." Republican presidential candidate Mitt Romney, a former governor of Massachusetts and a devout Mormon, was uniquely challenged during the 2008 campaign. (Mormons are people who belong to the Church of Jesus Christ of Latter-day Saints.) Not only did he have to convince voters of his ability to lead the country, but he also had to assure them that Mormonism is not a heretical cult, as some Christians apparently believed. "My view is that when a person of faith is running for office—particularly a faith you may not be familiar with—there are some questions that are legitimate," Romney told a writer for *Newsweek* in December 2007. Legitimate questions for voters to ask, Romney summarized, included: Would authorities of the candidate's church influence his decisions when he took office? And could a president of faith put America's traditions and laws above those of his church? Voters could rightfully expect a candidate to address those issues, Romney said, but other "theological concepts" did not need to be explained, regardless of one's faith.

Mike Huckabee, another candidate for the Republican nomination for president in the 2008 election, was an ordained Southern Baptist minister and former governor of Arkansas. He was also challenged during his campaign to defend his faith without criticizing other faiths. As the campaign was heating up in late 2007, reporters asked Huckabee what he thought of a speech Romney had delivered, in which he vowed to serve the interests of the United States over the interests of the Mormon Church. Huckabee replied, "I think it's a good thing and healthy for all of us … to discuss faith in the public square." However, when asked if he thought women should be ordained as ministers,

Massachusetts Governor Mitt Romney (*left*), a Mormon, and former Arkansas Governor Mike Huckabee, an ordained Southern Baptist minister, are pictured during a presidential debate in 2007.

a topic of concern to Southern Baptists, Huckabee declined to express his opinion. "It's so irrelevant to being president that I wouldn't even get into that," Huckabee said. Throughout the early days of the campaign, Huckabee consistently refused to discuss the details of his own religious beliefs beyond saying that he believed in God, Jesus, and the importance of values to the office of president.

A question posed to the nine Republican candidates for president during their first public debate on May 3, 2007, broadcast on television and over the internet, startled some viewers. A *Politico* reader submitted the question, "Do you believe in evolution?" Senator John McCain, who eventually secured the Republican nomination for president in the 2008 election, answered "yes," with the caveat, "But I also believe, when I hike the Grand Canyon and see it at sunset, that the hand of God is there also." Before the other eight candidates could answer the question, the debate moderator asked, "I'm curious, is there anybody on the stage that does not believe in evolution?" Three candidates—Senator Sam Brownback (Kansas), Huckabee, and Representative Tom Tancredo (Colorado)—raised their hands. The debate moderator then moved on to another question, effectively closing the evolution discussion. Some debate viewers barely noticed the question or the responses, while others were shocked and concerned. Shouldn't presidential hopefuls recognize evolution as a scientific fact, these viewers asked? Perhaps more to the point, should they even be required to answer such a question? Many viewers wondered whether the question itself was questionable, since it could be construed as a violation of the constitutional prohibition against religious tests for public office.

Calling for a Separation

Just as some Christians have sought to bring religion into the Constitution through changes in the Preamble, those on the other side of the separation of church and state argument have fought to keep religion out of government. In the 1870s and 1880s, groups who called themselves "secularists" and "liberals" organized a national campaign to obtain a constitutional amendment guaranteeing separation of church and state. Such amendments found little support in Congress or among the general population and were not passed. A leader in the effort, Francis Ellingwood Abbot, nonetheless founded a newspaper called the *Index* in 1870 that provided a forum for liberal views about the separation of church and state.

Abbot coined the term "liberalism," hoping that his allies would adopt it and unite under his leadership to become a politically effective group dedicated to the separation of church and state. In pursuit of this goal, Abbot published his "Nine Demands of Liberalism" in 1872, asking that "our entire political system shall be founded and administered on a purely secular basis." The "Demands" also specified:

- Church property should no longer be exempt from taxation.
- Chaplains in Congress, state legislatures, the military, and in prisons and other public institutions should no longer be employed by the government and paid with public funds.
- Public funds should no longer be used for religious education or charitable institutions.
- The use of the Bible in public schools should be prohibited.
- The president of the United States and all state governors should be prohibited from issuing proclamations for religious "festivals and fasts."
- The judicial oath in courts and other government departments that contain the phrase "under God" should be exchanged for those containing the simple affirmation, "under the pains and penalties of perjury."
- All laws enforcing the observance of Sunday as the Sabbath should be repealed.
- All laws should be structured to conform to rules of morality, equal rights, and liberty for all, rather than to "Christian" morality.
- There should be no privilege or advantage to Christianity or any other religion in the US Constitution and in state constitutions.

Abbot and his liberal followers did not succeed in changing the law or the Constitution with their list of demands. However, the debate concerning possible amendments to the constitution that would either strengthen or weaken the wall of separation between church and state has continued.

The fear that religion might have too much influence in the nation's public life has not been shared by all Americans, but was obviously prevalent in the latter years of the twentieth century. However, as Stephen L. Carter points out in *God's Name in Vain: The Wrongs and Rights of Religion in Politics*, the attitude that religion should have no place in politics would have put an end to the nineteenth-century abolition movement, which was led by Christian evangelicals who were mostly clergy and preached fiery sermons about a Christian's duty to love his neighbor as himself. The abolitionists preached that slavery was against the teachings of the Bible and that it was God's will for it to be abolished, regardless of the cost to slaveholders in the South. Furthermore, in the early twentieth century, when the industrial age was in full swing, men, women, and children worked at dangerous jobs for pennies a day and could be fired, beaten, arrested, and even murdered for trying to form unions. As Carter explains, religious people were among those who spoke out strongly against the widespread abuse of workers in the name of corporate profit and also helped bring about social change that included the push for public education, the battle for women's rights, the improvement of prisons and hospitals, and various crusades for world peace.

The Reverend Martin Luther King Jr. based his outspoken leadership of the civil rights movement in the mid-1960s on his religious beliefs, but his concern was for society's treatment of minorities in America, not for establishing his religion as the dominant faith. Human rights need not be confirmed by the state, he often argued, but were "God given." King worked for social change—an end to racial segregation in the United States—but he did it through the democratic process, and not through violence. "Let us march on ballot boxes," he said at the conclusion of the famous march from Selma to Montgomery, Alabama, in 1965, "until we send to our city councils, state legislatures, and the US

The Reverend Martin Luther King Jr., a US civil rights leader, is pictured during the March on Washington in 1963.

Congress, men who will not fear to do justice, love mercy, and walk humbly with their God."

Acting on Beliefs

People who act on their religious beliefs in political and governmental arenas can face pushback from secularists. "The problem goes well beyond our society's treatment of those who simply want freedom to worship in ways that most Americans find troubling," Carter wrote in *The Culture of Disbelief: How American Law and Politics Trivialize Religious Devotion*. "An analogous difficulty is posed by those whose religious convictions move them to action in the public arena." For example, when people who believe that God's will requires them to oppose abortion make their opposition known, others may complain that they are trying to impose their religious views on them. Furthermore, if the Supreme Court were to rule that abortion is illegal in the United States, many citizens would complain that religion had held too much sway over politics and had unduly influenced the Court's decision.

People who believe that their religious faith must guide all aspects of their lives may feel as though the wall of separation has become too intrusive on religious freedom in the United States. That wall has led to laws stating that members of the religious group Hare Krishna cannot solicit donations or sell religious material in airports; and that when lives are at stake, Jehovah's Witnesses must submit to blood transfusions even though their religion expressly prohibits them. The question then becomes whether such laws infringe on the rights of Americans to believe and worship as they please.

Federal tax laws, some Americans believe, also infringe on church members' rights to collectively participate in the political process. Part of the political process in America is the formation of various groups to advocate for their members' positions. When the groups give money to support certain candidates or legislation, they are called political action committees (PACs). As a group, church members may favor certain political candidates over others, but one disadvantage to becoming politically active for nonprofit religious groups and charities in the United States is that, according to federal tax law, if they publicly endorse or oppose political candidates they run the risk of losing their tax-exempt status. Because the government has consistently held that churches, religious groups, and charities provide benefits to society that the government does not provide, these groups have been exempt from paying income tax on donations and other income. They are also exempt from paying property tax or sales tax on products bought for use in religious worship, such as choir robes, hymnals, and so on. Even given these provisions, sometimes groups whose members advocate for certain candidates based on their religious views legally skirt tax-exemption laws by forming separate PACs and paying federal taxes on contributions to the groups.

Protecting Minorities

Carter wrote that the major religions practiced in the United States—mainstream Protestantism, Catholicism, and Judaism—generally receive adequate protection under the law. However, he added, "Religions that most need protection seem to receive it least." Native Americans, for instance, have seen their sacred lands systematically confiscated over several centuries for use by Christians and people of European descent. "Imagine the brouhaha," Carter says, "if New York City were to try to take St. Patrick's Cathedral by eminent domain to build a new convention center." They have been denied the use of peyote in their religious rituals because of anti-drug laws. In sum, "indigenous ritualistic religions are poorly understood and ill-protected under the First Amendment of the Constitution because practices, unlike beliefs, can be governmentally regulated," explained Stephanie Beran, a Nebraska attorney, in 2005. The American Indian Religious Freedom Act of 1978 sought to protect many practices that had once been legally prohibited.

Meanwhile, other religious minorities face discrimination, and their beliefs are even sometimes seen as contrary to the American political system. In 2017, Muslims comprised about 1 percent of the US population. A survey conducted by the Pew Research Center that year learned that 75 percent of Muslims reported "a lot" of anti-Muslim discrimination in the United States, and that such discrimination was on the rise. It's not difficult to see why they perceived the problem to be so pervasive: 41 percent of Americans polled said that Islam encourages violence more than other faiths do. What's more, 72 percent of white

Native Americans perform an Eagle Dance, a religious ceremony important to multiple tribes, in Taos, New Mexico.

evangelical Christians and 65 percent of Republicans believed that "Islam and democracy naturally conflict." Yet 92 percent of Muslims said they were proud to be Americans.

Some believe that one way to counter discrimination against minorities is to ensure that political representation reflects the demographic makeup of the country. Yet when it comes to religious makeup, Pew reports that in 2017, the 115th Congress resembled the legislative body as it was in the early 1960s. A total of 91 percent of members described themselves as Christian, whereas only 71 percent of US adults identify as Christian. Buddhists, Muslims, and Hindus were underrepresented, but most underrepresented of all were the religiously unaffiliated. While 23 percent of Americans identified as such, only one Congress member (0.2 percent of the legislative body) was unaffiliated.

Chapter Three

THE JUDICIAL BRANCH

Many landmark court cases concerning religious freedom and separation of church and state have reached the US Supreme Court, where nine justices usually decide matters involving the US Constitution. Such decisions have helped to define and limit religion's role in government. Cases typically reach the Supreme Court only after decisions are handed down in lower courts and either the plaintiffs or defendants appeal the decision. The Supreme Court justices decide which cases they will hear. Since the Supreme Court is the highest court in the nation, its decisions are final, although it may decide to return a case to a lower court for another hearing.

Opposite: Members of the United States Supreme Court are pictured in 1967. Thurgood Marshall (*top right*) was the court's newest member and first African American justice.

When laws are interpreted in courts, the prevailing judgment has been that, although a law may restrict some aspect of a religion, it is allowed to stand if the law is for the greater good.

For example, in 1899, the Supreme Court ruled that awarding a federal grant to a Roman Catholic organization for construction of a hospital did not violate the First Amendment, since people of all faiths would benefit. Similarly, in 1947, in *Everson v. Board of Education*, the court reviewed the rights of local school districts to provide free bus transportation to children attending parochial (religious) schools. After all arguments were heard, the court allowed the provision of transportation, determining that the bus transportation was a form of "public welfare legislation" that was being extended "to all its citizens without regard to their religious belief." However, Justice Hugo Black, who wrote the court's opinion, also recognized that "it approaches the verge" of the state's constitutional power. The court held:

The "establishment of religion" clause of the First Amendment means at least this: Neither a state nor the Federal Government can set up a church. Neither can pass laws which aid one religion, aid all religions, or prefer one religion over another. Neither can force nor influence a person to go to or to remain away from church against his will or force him to profess a belief or disbelief in any religion. No person can be punished for entertaining or professing religious beliefs or disbeliefs, for church attendance or non-attendance. No tax in any amount, large or small, can be levied to support any religious activities or institutions, whatever they may be called, or whatever form they may adopt to teach or practice religion. Neither a state nor the Federal

Government can, openly or secretly, participate in the affairs of any religious organizations or groups and vice versa. In the words of Jefferson, the clause against establishment of religion by law was intended to erect "a wall of separation" between church and State ... [The First] Amendment requires the state to be a neutral in its relations with groups of religious believers and non-believers; it does not require the state to be their adversary. State power is no more to be used so as to handicap religions than it is to favor them.

The Establishment Clause

In 1971, in *Lemon v. Kurtzman*, the Supreme Court's decision established a three-part test that became the standard for establishment-clause cases that followed. In deciding whether or not a state or federal law violated the establishment clause, the justices in this case focused on three points: sponsorship, financial support, and active involvement of the government in a religious activity. Under this test, a law would be constitutional only if it had a "secular purpose" (a purpose that is not religious), had a "primary effect" that neither advances nor inhibits religion, and did not create an "excessive government entanglement" with religion.

Applying this test, the justices in the *Lemon* case decided that a Pennsylvania law that allowed the state superintendent of public instruction to reimburse nonpublic schools, most of which were Catholic, for teachers' salaries, textbooks, and other instructional materials violated the establishment clause and was therefore unconstitutional.

The Supreme Court again applied the test devised in *Lemon* in a later decision. In 1969, Frederick Walz, a property owner in Richmond County, New York, had challenged property-tax

The Lemon Test

A Law Must …

1. **Have a secular legislative purpose**

2. **Not have the primary effect of either advancing or prohibiting religion**

3. **Not result in an "excessive government entanglement" with religion**

The Supreme Court's decision in the 1971 *Lemon v. Kurtzman* case set a standard test applicable to future establishment-clause cases.

exemptions for religious organizations on the grounds that such exemptions forced him, through his tax dollars, to contribute to religious organizations. In 1970, the Supreme Court decided in *Walz v. Tax Commission of City of New York* that New York's property tax exemptions for religious organizations were not unconstitutional. The court noted that tax exemptions for churches and other religious organizations were not required by the First Amendment's establishment clause, but argued that such exemptions are "deeply embedded in the fabric of our national life."

Furthermore, the court ruled that the New York legislature had a "secular legislative purpose" in granting the exemption, because it had "not singled out one particular church or religious group or even churches as such." Instead, the exemption was granted "to all houses of religious worship within a broad class of property owned by nonprofit, quasi-public corporations which

How Presidents Influence the Supreme Court

Since Supreme Court justices serve on the court for life, presidents are not often called upon to nominate a justice to replace one of the nine on the bench. Such job security within the government is reserved only for Supreme Court justices, to help ensure their independence from Congress and the president. Nominating a Supreme Court justice is one of a president's most important duties.

Article II, Section 2, Clause 2, of the Constitution says that the president "shall nominate, and by and with the Advice and Consent of the Senate, shall appoint … Judges of the Supreme Court." Once the Senate confirms the president's choice, the new justice is appointed. The president generally nominates a person he believes will decide cases in ways that agree with his administration's policies. For example, a liberal president may hope that Supreme Court decisions will reflect his strict separation of church and state views, while a conservative president may hope to see the justices lean toward allowing some crossover or collaboration between church and state.

When the political views of the president and the majority of the Senate differ greatly, appointing a new justice to the Supreme Court can be a difficult and lengthy process. Excellence and professionalism are the preferred qualities in nominees, but politics also influences the process. Between the appointment of the first justices in 1789 and 2006, the Senate confirmed 120 of the 154 nominated Supreme Court justices. President Barack Obama appointed two justices in 2009 and 2010—although his nomination of a third, in 2016, was stalled by Republican leaders in the Senate, allowing his successor to appoint one justice by 2018.

include hospitals, libraries, playgrounds, scientific, professional, historical, and patriotic groups." Also in line with the Lemon test, the exemption did not lead to government "entanglement" with religious groups.

In more recent decisions, the Supreme Court seemed increasingly willing to accommodate religion. For example, in *Marsh v. Chambers*, decided in 1983, the Court abandoned the tests used in *Lemon*, relying instead on historical custom when it upheld the widespread practice of saying prayers at the opening of state legislative sessions. Ernest Chambers, a Nebraska state legislator, had brought suit against the practice on the grounds that it constituted an establishment of religion. The Supreme Court's decision was that such practices are not unconstitutional, based on the fact that the practice has become "part of the fabric of our society." "It is," wrote Chief Justice Warren Burger, "simply a tolerable acknowledgment of beliefs widely held among the people of this country."

Supreme Court decisions reflect, to some extent, how many justices are liberal in their views and how many are conservative. In church-versus-state issues, a majority of liberal justices may mean that decisions most often reflect a strict separation of church and state, while if the majority of justices are conservative, decisions could lean more toward reducing the separation.

For example, in *Lynch v. Donnelly*, the court ruled on the constitutionality of the decision of Pawtucket, Rhode Island, to include a nativity scene reflecting events from the Christian Bible in its Christmas display in a shopping district. In addition to the nativity scene, the display included a Santa Claus house, a Christmas tree, and a banner wishing shoppers "Season's Greetings." Daniel Donnelly, a resident of Pawtucket, objected to the nativity scene being displayed on city property and filed suit against Pawtucket's mayor, Dennis Lynch. The Court held that, although the nativity scene had religious significance, the city was not attempting to establish a state church, and therefore had not violated the establishment clause. In writing the Court's majority opinion, the conservative Chief Justice Burger pointed out that it was "far too late in the day to impose a crabbed reading of the [establishment] Clause on the country."

The Free Exercise Clause

In addition to precedent-setting decisions concerning the establishment clause, the First Amendment's free exercise clause has also frequently been debated in the Supreme Court.

In 1940, in *Cantwell v. Connecticut*, the Supreme Court debated a case involving a Connecticut man, Newton Cantwell, and his two sons, Jesse and Russell, who were Jehovah's Witnesses. As required by their religion, the Cantwells had approached people on the street in a Catholic neighborhood to preach their religion and gone door-to-door to distribute religious literature. Two pedestrians voluntarily listened to an anti-Roman Catholic recording on the Cantwells' portable phonograph, then angrily reported the Cantwells to city authorities. The Cantwells were subsequently arrested for inciting a breach of the peace and for failing to acquire a permit required for solicitation. The Cantwells countercharged that the breach of peace and solicitation ordinances violated their rights of free speech and freedom of religion. The case eventually reached the Supreme Court.

In a unanimous decision, the court ruled in favor of the Cantwells. It held that, although general regulations on solicitation were legal, regulations that banned solicitation on religious grounds were not. The decision also emphasized that the First Amendment embraces two concepts—the freedom to believe as one chooses and the freedom to act, as long as the resultant actions are not a threat to society. While the Cantwells' message might have been offensive to some people, it did not threaten bodily harm and therefore was constitutionally protected religious speech.

In *Sherbert v. Verner*, argued in 1963, the Court sought to address the question of what types of religious actions would be allowed under the free exercise clause. Adeil Sherbert, a member of the Seventh-day Adventist Church, was fired from her job in a textile mill when she refused to work on Saturday, her religious Sabbath observance day. The South Carolina Employment Security Commission refused to accept Sherbert's religious reasons for her refusal to work on Saturdays and denied her unemployment compensation. The Supreme Court held that the South Carolina Employment Security Commission had violated Sherbert's First and Fourteenth Amendment rights, since the state's eligibility requirements for unemployment compensation placed a burden on Sherbert's ability to freely exercise her faith, and there was no compelling state interest to justify the burden. Therefore, Sherbert was eligible to receive unemployment benefits.

In recent years, the Supreme Court has moved toward neutrality in deciding establishment-clause and free exercise–clause cases. The court has often decided that when government regulations are valid and fairly applicable, they can't be overridden by accommodation for religious practices. *Employment Division, Department of Human Resources v. Smith* established this principle. The case was brought before the court by two Native Americans who were fired from their jobs as drug-rehabilitation counselors in Oregon because they took peyote for religious purposes. The two were denied unemployment compensation on the grounds that they were dismissed for job-related misconduct. The Oregon Supreme Court originally ruled that unemployment benefits should be paid because the state's interest in its compensation fund did not outweigh the burden placed on the plaintiffs' free exercise of religion. When the case first went before the US Supreme Court, it was returned to the state courts to determine whether the state's law against peyote as an illegal drug was constitutional. The Oregon courts ruled that it was, and the case returned to the Supreme Court, which upheld the Oregon decisions. The final verdict was that, since Oregon prohibits taking peyote but does not limit its prohibition just to Native Americans or to certain religions, the First Amendment had not been violated, and the state could deny unemployment benefits.

In another US Supreme Court decision, rendered in 1993, *Church of Lukumi Babalu Aye, Inc. v. City of Hialeah*, a law barring animal sacrifices was overturned because it targeted a specific religion by seeking to suppress specific religious practices. In the 1990s, the Church of Lukumi Babalu Aye, an Afro Caribbean–based Santería religion, established a branch in Hialeah, Florida. Followers of the Santería religion practice animal sacrifice as a form of worship, but the Hialeah city council passed several ordinances against using animal sacrifice in religious ceremonies. When the case reached the US Supreme Court, the court held that Hialeah's ordinances violated the First Amendment because they specifically targeted Santería religious practices. The decision meant that the members of the Church of Lukumi Babalu Aye could practice animal sacrifice, but the court stipulated that the sacrifices must be humanely performed.

The *Smith* and *Lukumi* decisions illustrate that if a law applies to everyone, has a compelling state interest such as taxation or following other constitutional laws, and does not specifically target religion in general or a specific religion, it probably does not violate Americans' First Amendment rights.

Deferring to the States

A more recent case illustrates the court's tendency to defer to state governments and to state and federal legislatures whenever possible when it comes to religious questions. In *Cutter v.*

Wilkinson, decided in 2005, the court considered whether or not the federal Religious Land Use and Institutionalized Persons Act (RLUIPA), passed in 2000, allowed prison inmates to practice nonmainstream religions without violating the First Amendment antiestablishment provision. Section 3 of the act says in part, "No government shall impose a substantial burden on the religious exercise of a person residing in or confined in an institution," unless the burden furthers "a compelling government interest" and does so by the "least restrictive means."

Several current and former prisoners in a federal prison in Ohio brought suit before RLUIPA was passed, alleging that they were not allowed the same free exercise of their religions as prisoners who practiced mainstream religions. The prisoners who sued followed Asatru (a form of paganism), Satanism, Wicca, and the Church of Jesus Christ Christian. The various prison officials listed as defendants claimed as a defense that RLUIPA unconstitutionally advanced religion, thus violating the First Amendment's establishment clause.

Head santera Carmen Pal (*center*) leads a Santería religious service in Hialeah, Florida, in 1987.

The court, disagreeing with a lower court of appeals, found that the law did not violate the establishment clause. The published decision said, in part:

> The Religion Clauses of the First Amendment provide: "Congress shall make no law respecting an establishment of religion, or prohibiting the free exercise thereof." The first of the two Clauses, commonly called the Establishment Clause, commands a separation of church and state. The second, the Free Exercise Clause, requires government respect for, and noninterference with, the religious beliefs and practices of our Nation's people. While the two Clauses express complementary values, they often exert conflicting pressures.

Their decision, the justices said, recognizes that "there is room for play in the joints between the clauses, some space for legislative action neither compelled by the Free Exercise Clause nor prohibited by the Establishment Clause."

Although it seemed to hinge on a technicality, the decision in *Cutter v. Wilkinson* effectively guaranteed the rights of prison inmates to practice their religion and prompted this remark from Brian Fahling, senior legal counsel for the American Family Association, a group whose members generally take a conservative view on the separation of church and state: "It is a sign of the times, I suppose, that it took a Witch and a Satanist to secure the rights of inmates to worship."

These and many more Supreme Court decisions have set precedents for state and federal courts to follow in the future as they decide cases. The first decades of the twenty-first century have seen a move toward states' rights to interpret the First

Amendment. They have also seen key decisions as the debate continues, such as the unanimous 2009 decision against a church that argued that if the municipality of Pleasant Grove, Utah, could erect a privately donated Ten Commandments monument on public property, the church should be allowed to erect its own, similarly sized monument. Questions of taxpayer funding for private, parochial schools have also come before the court, as in 2011, when the court ruled 5–4 against Arizona taxpayers who argued that tax credits for people who donate to private or religious school scholarships violated the establishment clause. As of 2018, five out of four Supreme Court justices were generally considered more conservative, which might have an impact on future separation of church and state decisions.

Chapter Four

RELIGION IN THE PUBLIC SCHOOLS

From questions regarding when and if prayer should be permitted in public schools to whether religious concepts should be presented in science classrooms, public schools have been one of the most prominent battlegrounds in the debate over separation of church and state.

As Stephen M. Feldman observes in *Please Don't Wish Me a Merry Christmas: A Critical History of the Separation of Church and State*, the 1950s marked a period of "religious fervor" in the United States and launched many of the issues that are still being played out in the political arena and in the courts today. "Both old and novel practices that intermingled religion and government were the norm." The phrase "under God" was added to the Pledge of

Opposite: South Carolina first-graders are pictured during a silent, in-school prayer in 1966.

Allegiance. The Supreme Court opened its daily sessions with the invocation "God save the United States and this honorable Court." American currency proclaimed, "In God We Trust." Christian symbols and figures, such as crucifixes, crèches, and representations of the Ten Commandments were increasingly displayed in public places—sometimes on government property.

On the education front, every Wednesday afternoon, public schoolchildren in some communities were released from classes if (and only if) they attended Christian-education classes. Sometimes the religious classes were not held on school campuses, but in church meeting rooms, and other times they were held in the public school building. In many schools, Bible readings, daily prayers, and classroom celebrations of Christmas and Easter were common school activities.

School Prayer

In what seemed to be a reasonable suggestion at the time, given the religious activities practiced throughout America's public schools, the Board of Regents of New York State recommended in 1951 that school boards have children recite a prayer each day in school in order to further moral values and religious education. The Regents recommended that students recite the following "nondenominational" prayer: "Almighty God, we acknowledge our dependence upon Thee, and we beg Thy blessings upon us, our parents, our teachers and our Country."

When the school board in New Hyde Park, Long Island, adopted the prayer for use in local schools in 1958, several parents sued the school district, claiming that the recitation of the prayer in the public schools was unconstitutional. The Supreme Court decided the case *Engel v. Vitale* in 1962, holding that the daily recitation of the Regents' prayer in public schools violated the establishment clause of the First Amendment and was therefore unconstitutional. The decision drew upon Protestant history, recalling that one reason the Puritans fled England in the seventeenth century was to escape the governmentally imposed *Book of Common Prayer* used in the Church of England, the nationally sanctioned religion in England at that time. *Engel v. Vitale* became precedent for school prayer decisions.

The first Supreme Court case to be decided in 1963, *Abington School District v. Schempp*, involved school prayer and Bible reading in Pennsylvania public schools. At the beginning of the school day, students were required to read at least ten Bible verses from the King James Version of the Bible. Afterward, students were to recite, in unison, the Lord's Prayer, followed by the Pledge of Allegiance. Students could be excused from the Bible reading and prayer with a written note from their parents. A group of parents asked the school board to rescind the rule, and when they would not, a lawsuit was filed; it eventually reached the Supreme Court. The Supreme Court found that the requirement was, indeed, a violation of students' First and Fourteenth Amendment rights. The fact that students could be excused with written notes from parents was irrelevant, the decision stated, since the schools' requirement violated the establishment clause.

Another case involving mandatory school prayer, *Murray v. Curlett*, was filed in 1959, and, because of similarities with *Abington*, the two cases were decided together in 1963. *Murray v. Curlett* involved the outspoken atheist Madalyn Murray (she later remarried and became Madalyn Murray O'Hare), who founded a group called the American Atheists Association in 1963. In 1959, Murray enrolled her son in elementary school in Baltimore, Maryland, where students were required to read the Bible and pray in unison before classes began. Murray wrote an excuse for her son not to participate, which school policy allowed her to do. Murray's son was told to sit in the hallway while his classmates read the Bible and prayed, which, Murray protested, singled him out as different from his classmates and subjected him to ridicule and abuse. The school board refused to change the rule, and Murray filed a lawsuit.

The Supreme Court justices in the *Abington* and *Murray* cases made it clear in their published decision that the state was to remain neutral in matters pertaining to religion. Justice Tom C. Clark wrote in his decision: "In light of the history of the First Amendment and of our cases interpreting and applying its requirements, we hold that the practices at issue and the laws requiring them are unconstitutional under the Establishment Clause."

The precedent established in *Abington School District v. Schempp* and *Murray v. Curlett* has not been overturned. Public school districts across the nation have generally refrained from requiring or allowing prayers to be spoken aloud in classrooms and in school-sponsored activities, but silent, personal prayer has not and will not be prohibited. In short, the courts have ruled unconstitutional any prayer that is sponsored, led, sanctioned, scheduled, or encouraged by the government.

When court decisions made it clear that public schools could not require or schedule student prayer, some school districts implemented a "moment of silence," usually in the morning before classes began, during which children could pray silently if they wished. Alabama passed a law in 1978 that mandated a "minute of silent meditation" at the beginning of the school day, but in 1981, the law was changed to read "silent meditation or prayer." In *Wallace v. Jaffree*, a parent challenged the revised law, alleging that it was unconstitutional because it forced students to pray, therefore exposing them to religious indoctrination. Lower courts allowed the school district's moment of silence to stand as written, but on appeal the case reached the US Supreme Court. In a 6–3 decision, the court found the Alabama law to be in violation of the First Amendment's establishment clause. The court held that the words "or prayer" being added to the law were simply an attempt to return voluntary prayer to the classroom.

Despite these Supreme Court decisions, many school districts continued to include prayer in school activities through the 1970s. Then, in the 1980s and 1990s, legal challenges to prayer during school activities multiplied. The decisions in lower courts were, however, mixed. For example, in one Virginia jurisdiction, a court ruled that organized graduation prayers could be said (*Grossberg v. Deusebio*, 1974). Yet a court in another jurisdiction in California reached the opposite conclusion, even though the prayers were interdenominational and voluntary (*Bennett v. Livermore Unified School District*, 1987). Therefore, it would seem that whether or not prayers at public school graduation ceremonies met constitutional standards depended on where the school happened to be located.

In *Brown v. Gilmore*, in 2001, another example of lower-court decisions added to the confusion regarding prayer in public schools; a Virginia statute that made a daily moment of silence mandatory in every public school in the commonwealth was declared not to be a violation of the First Amendment. The law's "intent" is clear, the Fourth Circuit Court held—to establish a moment of silence in school during which silent prayer is but one option available to students.

Even after prayer in public school classrooms had been declared unconstitutional, most public schools continued to allow it at traditional school ceremonies such as commencements and athletic events. But this practice, too, was challenged legally.

In *Lee v. Weisman*, the Supreme Court heard arguments for and against prayer at commencement exercises. In 1991, Robert Lee, a middle-school principal in Providence, Rhode Island, invited a rabbi to speak at his school's graduation ceremony. Daniel Weisman's daughter was a member of the graduating class, and he filed a request for a temporary restraining order to prevent the rabbi from speaking. The court denied Weisman's request, but after the graduation ceremony, where prayers were recited, Weisman requested a permanent restraining order to keep Providence school officials from inviting clergy to deliver invocations and benedictions at school ceremonies. The Supreme Court decided the case in 1992, holding that the inclusion of clergy who offer prayers in official school ceremonies violates the establishment clause of the First Amendment.

If prayer in classrooms and at school ceremonies and activities is unconstitutional, some school officials reasoned, then surely student-sanctioned and student-led prayer is not. This question was decided by *Santa Fe Independent School District v. Doe* in 2000. Prior to 1995, a student elected as Santa Fe High School's student council chaplain delivered a Christian prayer over the public-address system before each home varsity football game. One Mormon and one Catholic family filed suit, challenging this practice under the establishment clause of the First Amendment.

While the suit was pending in a district court, the school district adopted a new policy that permitted, but did not require, student-initiated and student-led prayer at all the home games. The new policy also authorized two student votes: the first to

Football players at Odessa High School in Odessa, Texas, are pictured praying after a game in 2000.

determine whether "invocations" should be delivered at games and the second to select the spokesperson to deliver them. After the students authorized such prayers and selected a spokesperson, the district court entered an order modifying the policy to permit only nonsectarian, nonproselytizing prayer.

The plaintiffs appealed the district court's order, and a court of appeals held that, even as modified by the district court, the football prayer policy was invalid. The school district claimed that its policy did not violate the establishment clause because the football game prayers were private student speech, not public speech.

The US Supreme Court agreed to hear the case, and in a 6–3 decision, held that the football game prayers, even though they were student-sanctioned and student-led, took place on government property at government-sponsored events and, as a result, were not private speech but public speech. They were therefore a violation of the First Amendment's establishment clause.

Supreme Court decisions have set important precedents for lower courts to follow when judging cases involving religion in the public schools, and have provided guidelines for school districts when considering whether or not to allow prayer and other forms of worship at school functions. They have not, however, resolved the argument in the minds of those parents, educators, students, and others who feel strongly about the issue.

Those who oppose prayer and other religious activities in public schools maintain that proponents have confused the state's neutral stance with hostility. Religion or lack of religion is a private matter, this side argues, and its instruction and practice should be left to parents in the privacy of their homes or religious leaders in their places of worship. Others decry the absence of prayer in public schools and argue that the Supreme Court has taken too hard a stance against the freedom of public school students to pray when and how they want.

Religion in Science Classrooms

Prayer is not the only separation of church and state issue affecting the American public school system. Some Christians' criticism of public schools centers on the charges that they promote anti-Christian values and that they prevent parents from teaching their children values based on religion. For instance, those Christians who believe the Bible to be true in all respects object to the public schools' choice to teach evolution in science classes. Others believe that abstaining from sexual activity should be the only choice as their children mature sexually, and they object to schools' attempts to teach safe-sex practices that involve the use of condoms and birth-control pills. Some people do not want other religions taught as equal to Christianity, and some don't want alternative families, such as those headed by gay or lesbian parents, to be mentioned in classrooms at all. For nearly every intersection of religion in schools and the law, there are people who object.

The Scopes Trial

Some parents have given up on public schools and choose to educate their children at home or to send them to religious schools. Others have become active in battles to change public school curricula. The teaching of evolution in science classes is particularly unpopular among those Christians who believe in a literal interpretation of the Bible. The evolution issue was first tackled in court in 1925, in the now-famous *Tennessee v. Scopes* trial. Journalists called it "the trial of the century" because it pitted Clarence Darrow and William Jennings Bryan, two famous attorneys of the day, against one another. Newspapers also nicknamed it "the monkey trial," referring to the evolutionary theory that people evolved from apes.

John Thomas Scopes, a teacher in Dayton, Tennessee, was accused of violating a state law against teaching evolution instead of creationism in public schools. Local activists had encouraged Scopes to teach evolution as a deliberate test of the constitutionality of the state's antievolution law. Scopes's attorney was Clarence Darrow, a successful trial lawyer, an agnostic (one who neither believes nor disbelieves in the existence of God), and a longtime opponent of teaching creationism as fact. Prosecutor William Jennings Bryan, also a well-known attorney and a three-time candidate for president, opposed the teaching of evolution in public schools and believed in a literal interpretation of the Bible.

In the stifling July heat, in Rhea County Courthouse in Dayton, Tennessee, the two attorneys battled. A jury of twelve mostly middle-aged men, consisting of farmers and churchgoers, heard the case. The defense sought not to have Scopes acquitted, but to get a ruling from a higher court, preferably the US Supreme Court, that Tennessee's antievolution law was unconstitutional. Darrow was not allowed to pursue this line of defense, so he relied instead on his argument that "civilization" was on trial against religious zealots who would make the Bible "every man's" last word. Bryan pointed to the book of Genesis from the King James version of the Bible to bolster his side of the argument. Bryan also

Lawyers Clarence Darrow (*left*) and William Jennings Bryan faced off during the famous 1925 Scopes trial over the teaching of evolution.

took the stand as a witness for the prosecution and an expert on the Bible, stumbling under Darrow's relentless questioning. At one point, Bryan answered, "I do not think about things I don't think about." Darrow then asked, "Do you think about things you do think about?" When Bryan responded, "Well, sometimes," the spectators laughed.

In his closing speech, Darrow asked the jury to return a guilty verdict against his client in order to allow an appeal to the Tennessee Supreme Court. The jury complied, and a year later the Tennessee Supreme Court reversed the decision on a technicality, but not on the constitutional grounds for which Darrow had hoped. Five days after the trial was over, William Jennings Bryan died.

Kitzmiller v. Dover School District

The Dover, Pennsylvania school board decided in October 2004 to require ninth-grade biology students to hear a brief statement at the start of the semester saying that there were "gaps" in the theory of evolution, that the concept of "intelligent design" was an alternative, and that students could learn more about it by reading a textbook, *Of Pandas and People*, available in the high-school library. Intelligent design is the belief that some organisms are so complex that natural evolutionary selection cannot fully account for them. But the board had not anticipated the furor that the decision would cause. In December 2004, eleven parents, represented by the American Civil Liberties Union (ACLU), Americans United for Separation of Church and State (AU), and a private law firm sued the school board, alleging violation of the separation of church and state, since, the group maintained, intelligent design is a religious concept.

As the first school board in the United States to introduce the concept of intelligent design in science classes, the Dover board became the center of national media attention. The trial concluded

Key Decisions on Teaching Evolution

In 1925, while the Scopes trial was making headlines, fifteen states had passed laws against teaching evolution in public schools. As time passed, the laws were seldom enforced, but their constitutionality was not effectively challenged until *Epperson v. Arkansas* in 1968.

Susan Epperson, a young woman with a master's degree in zoology, taught high school biology in Little Rock, Arkansas. Epperson was asked to teach from a textbook that included a section on evolution. Since Arkansas still had a 1925 antievolution statute on its books, Epperson faced a dilemma. If she taught from the required textbook, she could possibly face criminal charges and dismissal (although Arkansas was not actively enforcing its antievolution statute). To solve her dilemma, Epperson challenged the law in a state court. The court decided that Arkansas's antievolution law was unconstitutional because it violated the free speech provision of the First Amendment.

Since some parents believed that teaching evolution, which presents theories on the origin of human beings that differ from biblical accounts, was counter to their religious beliefs, they continued to push to include creationism in curricula as an alternative to evolution. In some areas the push was successful. In 1987, however, the US Supreme Court ruled in *Edwards v. Aguillard* that states cannot require public schools to balance evolution lessons by teaching creationism. The decision was in response to a 1981 Louisiana state law whose supporters claimed that the bill's secular purpose was "protecting academic freedom." High-school teacher Don Aguillard and other opponents filed suit, arguing that the law violated the establishment clause. The court used the Lemon test (explained in Chapter Three) to conclude that the law, commonly referred to as the Creationism Act, was attempting to advance a religious belief.

on November 4, 2005, with the decision that intelligent design is a religious concept and that teaching it in schools violates the establishment clause of the First Amendment. US district judge John E. Jones delivered a stinging opinion against the Dover school district, holding that the district had violated the Constitution's First Amendment. Jones's ruling stated that intelligent design "is a religious view, a mere re-labeling of creationism, and not a scientific theory." Jones also criticized the "breathtaking inanity" of the Dover action and accused several school board members of lying to conceal their true motive, which was to promote religion. The Dover school district members who instituted the measure were voted out of office.

In 2005, when President George W. Bush said that he believed schools should teach both the theories of evolution and intelligent design, those in favor of teaching intelligent design were encouraged. However, after the Dover decision, many states issued mandates against teaching intelligent design or creationism in public school science classes. Some state education boards (e.g., Kansas) recommended teaching "doubts" about the certainty of evolution, which supporters praised as "a victory for free speech" and opponents criticized as "shabby politics and worse science."

The School Voucher Debate

In recent decades, the school voucher debate has been at the forefront of the separation of church and state issue in education. As of 2017, school vouchers or similar programs were available in nearly thirty states. School vouchers essentially redirect government funds from public to private schools, allowing students to use taxpayer money that would have funded their public school education in order to attend private schools, which are sometimes religious schools. The latter are considered good alternatives by many parents who oppose the lack of religious instruction in public institutions. Others argue that such voucher programs are particularly beneficial for low-income students who are receiving a poor public education. However, the other side of the debate insists that redirecting these funds systematically undercuts public education's ability to succeed by underfunding it and encouraging flight from—rather than rehabilitation of—underperforming schools. What's more, in those cases in which students opt to attend religious schools, voucher opponents argue that government is essentially subsidizing religious instruction.

The debate on school choice—a broader issue that includes choice between different types of public schools and questions around tax credit scholarship programs and other initiatives—came to a head in 2017, when Donald Trump nominated Betsy DeVos as US education secretary. DeVos, a billionaire philanthropist and Republican donor, had no experience working as an educator; rather, she was an outspoken school-choice advocate. In her first year heading the US Department of Education, DeVos focused on investing in "individual students, not systems." She sought funding for charter schools and public school vouchers, but as of late 2017, most of her requests had been ignored by Congress, and it remains unclear whether new federal laws may be put in place that impact school voucher programs in the future.

President Donald Trump (*left*) is pictured alongside Betsy DeVos (*center*), a controversial pick for US education secretary in 2017.

Chapter Five

SOCIAL BEHAVIOR AND THE LAW

Because offenses such as murder, theft, and assault are prohibited by many religious texts, such as the Torah, the Quran, and the Bible, many governments throughout history have drawn direct links between their laws and the religious principles that they resemble. This was common in colonial America, but the Founding Fathers argued that the law could prohibit such offenses on a moral basis independent of religious ties. Still, throughout the nation's history, it has often proven difficult to disentangle religious concerns from moral and legal ones.

In colonial America, criminals were those who committed murder or beat or robbed their neighbors, but in seventeenth-century Boston, anyone who

Opposite: People considered to be evildoers during the American colonial era were placed in stocks for punishment, as was the case for this man, shown in a Boston square circa 1657.

"willfully blasphemes the name of God" was also labeled a criminal. Just as murderers and thieves could be jailed or put to death, blasphemers could be confined to wooden stocks in the public square and pelted with rotten fruit and vegetables. They could also be jailed, whipped, or otherwise punished. (Blasphemers were those who spoke God's name in vain, or otherwise made disparaging remarks about religion.)

The Temperance Movement

By the nineteenth and twentieth centuries, many laws inspired by religion were considerably softened or were no longer enforced. Laws governing moral conduct, however, were still a part of American society. For example, throughout the 1800s, several groups spearheaded movements to abolish alcohol based on the belief that drunkenness caused poverty, cultivated violence, fostered disease, and was a threat to

Women's Christian Temperance Union members drain barrels of liquor seized during 1929 raids. At the time, selling alcohol was illegal.

marriages and the family. In 1826, the American Temperance Society was founded to convince people to stop drinking alcoholic beverages. The Woman's Christian Temperance Union (WCTU) joined the ranks of temperance organizations in 1873. WCTU members stood outside saloons singing hymns and reading the Bible. They also preached observance of the Sabbath and visited prisoners in jail to encourage moral behavior and abstinence from alcohol. Members of the WCTU were joined in their fight to abolish alcohol in 1893 by the all-male members of the Anti-Saloon League, who advocated for the enforcement of existing temperance laws, as well as new legislation to outlaw alcoholic beverages.

In 1919, the temperance movement culminated in the ratification of the Eighteenth Amendment to the Constitution, which mandated Prohibition, making it illegal to manufacture, transport, and sell alcoholic beverages. Congress passed the Volstead Act in 1919, allowing the government to enforce provisions of the Eighteenth Amendment. Prohibition proved impossible to enforce, however, due to widespread bootlegging (making and selling liquor illegally), flouting of the law, and federal underfunding for enforcement. In fact, organized crime flourished during Prohibition due to widespread involvement in bootlegging and running "speakeasies" (clandestine bars where liquor was sold illegally). The speakeasies promoted not only drinking, but also gambling, prostitution, and tobacco use. By 1933, the Eighteenth Amendment was considered a lost cause and the Twenty-First Amendment, repealing Prohibition, was passed.

The Prohibition era (1920–1933) ushered in additional laws governing moral behavior. It was illegal to sell cigarettes in some states, and in some locations, there was strict local censorship of books, films, plays, and other forms of entertainment. Antiprostitution laws were already on the books in most communities, but after Prohibition ended, they were more stridently enforced. (Despite laws against prostitution, however, the practice continues throughout the United States. Nevada is the only state that has legalized prostitution, and in that state, prostitutes must be periodically tested for sexually transmitted and other communicable diseases and must pay income taxes.)

Sabbatarian laws, such as the prohibition against retail and alcohol sales on Sunday, have remained in effect in many American communities through the twentieth and into the twenty-first centuries, but they are often so honeycombed with exceptions that they are seldom enforced.

The Abortion Debate

Modern societal moral and ethical debates—and related legislation and court challenges—center more around abortion; homosexuality and the rights of the LGBTQ community; and other topics, such as scientific research that involves the use of human embryos. When federal and state governments pass laws regulating these topics, the laws may be challenged as violations of the separation of church and state if people perceive them as based on religious beliefs. The Supreme Court case around which the current controversy over abortion centers is *Roe v. Wade*. Since many people oppose abortion on religious grounds, some consider laws that regulate or prohibit abortion a violation of the separation of church and state.

Roe v. Wade involved twenty-one-year-old Norma McCorvey, a Dallas, Texas resident, who became pregnant in 1969. She was divorced at the time, and her parents were raising her young child. McCorvey was having trouble finding work because of her pregnancy, and she dreaded the stigma attached to an illegitimate birth. She looked for a physician who would perform an abortion but was unsuccessful, because at that time, Texas was one of forty-six states that had laws against abortion. The Texas law had

Pro-life and pro-choice demonstrators are pictured outside a Little Rock, Arkansas, abortion clinic in 1994.

been passed in 1859 and was similar to antiabortion laws in other states in that it targeted for prosecution those who performed abortions, not the women who requested them.

During her search for an abortion provider, McCorvey met two attorneys, Sarah Weddington and Linda Coffee, who wanted to challenge the state's antiabortion law, and she agreed to file a lawsuit under the fictitious name "Jane Roe." The class action lawsuit, representing all pregnant women in Texas, was filed against Henry Wade, the district attorney in Dallas County,

Texas. The suit alleged that Jane Roe had limited rights to an abortion. It asked the court to find the Texas antiabortion law unconstitutional.

On appeal, the Roe case reached the US Supreme Court, where it was decided in 1973. (In the meantime, Norma McCorvey gave birth, and the child was put up for adoption.) The court held that the Texas law was unconstitutional, not because it violated the separation of church and state, but because of the Fourteenth Amendment's "due process clause." The clause states, in part: "No state shall make or enforce any law which shall abridge the privileges or immunities of citizens of the United States; nor shall any State deprive any person of life, liberty, or property, without due process of law." In short, the court decided that the Constitution protects privacy, and that it should therefore be legal for a woman to make the private decision of whether or not to have an abortion, for any reason, during the first two trimesters (six months) of the pregnancy. States could impose restrictions and regulate abortions after that. (In 2003, Congress passed a law banning "partial birth" abortions in the United States—those taking place during the second or third trimesters of a pregnancy.)

The decision in *Roe v. Wade* made history, because it made abortion legal in the United States during the first six months of a pregnancy. Since the decision, many states have passed laws that restrict abortion rights. However, ballot initiatives in South Dakota and Colorado that would have strongly limited such rights were soundly defeated in November 2008. By 2018, a twenty-week abortion ban had been enacted in twenty-one states and blocked in two. The US Senate, however, blocked a similar measure on January 29, 2018.

In the unlikely event that the Supreme Court ever overturns *Roe v. Wade*, some states may immediately enact laws to once again make abortion illegal, while other states may pass laws making abortion legal in that state, regardless of federal law. Since *Roe v. Wade*, groups on both sides of the issue have loudly asserted their views. There are two main positions on the antiabortion, or "pro-life" side:

1. Mainstream pro-life advocates believe that abortion should only be legal in cases of rape, incest, or when the pregnancy endangers the mother's life. If *Roe v. Wade* should be overturned, it is possible that the mainstream pro-life position would prevail.

2. Absolutist pro-life advocates are more likely to take the position that abortion should never be legal, and individuals on this side of the issue are sometimes fanatical in their views. For instance, Planned Parenthood facilities—most of which no longer provide abortion services—have frequently been harassed as antiabortion groups and individuals picket outside their doors and shout curses at women who go there seeking medical advice. In some cases, antiabortion fanatics have bombed offices where they believe abortions take place, resulting in laws that require protesters to stay a certain distance away from the facilities. Lists of physicians suspected of performing abortions, including their addresses, have been posted on the Internet, and some physicians have been injured and even killed by absolutist pro-lifers.

Evangelicals and traditional Catholics generally take the pro-life side of the abortion issue, arguing that taking a human life is never defensible. Most people of faith, however, do not condone the hate and violence that the abortion issue sometimes inspires.

The pro-choice side of the abortion issue holds that a woman should have free choice over whether or not to bear a child, regardless of the circumstances of conception. Mainstream pro-choice advocates do not support abortion very late in a healthy pregnancy, but rather support the *Roe v. Wade* decision that states can't ban abortion prior to the viability of the child—that is, its

The Religious Coalition for Reproductive Choice

Just when we think we have it straight—placing liberals, Democrats, and nonreligious people on one side of the argument over abortion, and conservatives, Republicans, and churchgoers on the opposite side—a story like the following appears in the media.

The Religious Coalition for Reproductive Choice (RCRC) is a group whose members are religious, but also pro-choice on matters of reproduction, such as abortion and birth control. "We are not pro-choice in spite of our faith, we are pro-choice because our faith instructs us," said seminarian Kelli Clement in an article that appeared in the March 4, 2008, issue of the *Minnesota Monitor*. Clement, a member of the Unitarian Universalist Church, had an abortion when she was in her twenties and addicted to alcohol, which can endanger the health of a fetus. "I have never regretted my choice to terminate that pregnancy. It was the most loving thing I could do," she said.

Clement said that religious individuals who take a more "nuanced" view might come to see the abortion issue as separate from their religious beliefs, as she does. "We need to become comfortable with ... a broader, more liberal view of God."

The RCRC remains active to this day. In January 2018, RCRC members joined four Christian pastors and a rabbi to bless a Maryland abortion clinic.

ability to survive outside the womb. Their argument is based on several key positions:

1. Women have a right to decide what happens to their own bodies, protected by their constitutional right to privacy.
2. The right to have an abortion supports gender equality, given that women suffer more personal and professional obstacles than men do when they become parents. In turn, it breaks cycles of poverty, giving low-income women and families the choice not to have children if they can't afford to do so.
3. Making abortion illegal puts women at risk of injury or death by forcing many to seek out illegal abortions, which are often carried out without the proper medical training, facilities, or tools in place. In 1965, before *Roe v. Wade*, one in six of all childbirth- and pregnancy-related deaths were caused by illegal abortions.

Same-Sex Marriage and LGBTQ Rights

Mainstream religions vary greatly in their policies toward homosexuality. Some view it as a sin but emphasize that condemnation applies to the sexual act only, and not to the people concerned. Other groups believe homosexuals can be converted to heterosexuality through prayer and religious intervention. Followers of some religions or orders may believe that only heterosexual marriages should be legal, although some Christian churches now readily accept gay ministers. Attempts to pass a constitutional amendment proclaiming marriage as the union between one man and one woman have failed in the United States, but in 1996, the US Congress passed the Defense of Marriage Act (DOMA). The act denied federal recognition of same-sex

Supporters of LGBTQ rights celebrate in California on June 26, 2015, after the US Supreme Court legalized same-sex marriage.

marriages and gave each state the right to refuse to recognize same-sex marriage licenses obtained in other states.

The last several years, however, have seen a significant expansion of same-sex marriage rights in the United States. On June 26, 2013, the Supreme Court ruled that same-sex spouses who have been legally married are eligible to receive federal benefits, overruling parts of DOMA. These benefits include naming a same-sex partner as the spouse for health insurance coverage and for receiving the pension benefits of the deceased or divorced partner. The years after saw a wave of legalization in such states as New Jersey, Hawaii, Illinois, and more courts rejecting state-level bans on same-sex marriage in such states as Arkansas, Idaho, Arizona, South Carolina, Montana, and Oklahoma. On June 26, 2015, a 5–4 US Supreme Court ruling legalized gay marriage nationwide. In 2017, 62 percent of Americans were in favor of same-sex marriage, according to the Pew Research Center.

Even so, same-sex marriage is not the only issue of concern to the LGBTQ community and its supporters. In the last few years, debates over transgender rights have sparked controversy regarding laws prohibiting people from using the restroom associated with their gender identity. (A transgender person is someone who has a gender identity inconsistent with the sex they were assigned at birth.) At least twenty-four states considered such legislation between 2013 and 2016; North Carolina became the only state to enact it, and faced significant backlash for doing so on the national stage. In 2017, at least sixteen more states considered similar laws, and at least fourteen considered bills that would restrict the rights of transgender students at school.

Some religious groups, in seeking to institute these restrictions, argue that being transgender violates scripture and natural law, but the LGBTQ community argues that they should not be legally obligated to hide who they are. Transgender rights have seen a few wins so far in the courts. In response to Trump's efforts to prevent transgender troops from joining the military, a federal district court ruled in October 2017 that such a ban violates constitutional rights and mandated that transgender recruits would be formally permitted to enlist as of January 1, 2018. Also, several circuit court decisions have ruled discrimination against transgender people in the workplace unlawful. Even so, transgender people still face discrimination and a rise in violent hate crimes; at least twenty-five transgender individuals were killed in 2017, according to the Human Rights Campaign.

Since the founding of the United States, religious citizens have been an influential force in society, encouraging moral behavior and advocating for laws to regulate humanity's more primitive instincts. The future relationship of church and state, however, remains unclear, as rapid societal changes, technological advancements, globalization, and immigration change the demographics of countries around the world and introduce new ideas, many of which challenge traditional religious beliefs and the role that different religions should play—or not play—in government.

Chapter Six

RELIGIOUS UNDERSTANDING IN FOREIGN AFFAIRS

When negotiating, collaborating, or even warring with other countries, it is essential to understand not only their political perspectives, but also their cultural and religious heritage. Only in recent decades has US foreign policy shifted to encompass religious understanding as key to formulating well-informed policies and cultivating meaningful international relationships. In many ways, the United States and its leaders have had to learn a great deal more about other religions in order to achieve this.

The question arises from the two schools of thought that the US government uses in dealing with other nations. The so-called idealistic school of thought concerning America's foreign policy contends that

Opposite: Members of terrorist organization the Islamic State of Iraq and the Levant (ISIL) march in a propaganda video. ISIL, also called ISIS, bases its dogma on an aberrant version of Islam.

all forms of interaction between countries—economic, as in trade; militaristic, as in police actions and military bases; diplomatic, as in official visits and treaties; and social, as in tourism and extended visits—must at some point take place between people. And if people are concerned about the welfare of others, an attitude that is allegedly established by religious teachings, this will be reflected in dealings with other nations.

This manner of looking at foreign relations derives from the traditional belief of Americans that their country is exceptional—a beacon of freedom and enlightenment for less-developed nations. This viewpoint encourages Americans to become missionaries—both in the religious sense, in bringing Christianity to people in other nations, and in the political sense, in encouraging the spread of democracy worldwide.

A second school of thought among foreign policy analysts—realism—cautions against believing that nations will behave like people. Dean Acheson, who served as President Harry S. Truman's secretary of state, subscribed to this school of thought. He wrote in 1964, "A good deal of trouble comes from the anthropomorphic urge to regard nations as individuals and apply to our own national conduct, for instance, the Golden Rule—even though in practice individuals rarely adopt it. The fact is that nations are not individuals; the cause and effect of their actions are wholly different." Nations, this premise holds, will always behave to secure their own interests, with no regard for the morality of their actions.

Over time, the United States' foreign policy has been a mixture of these two schools of thought, sometimes concerned with spreading democracy and with moral principles such as human rights, and other times forced to be realistic, as when siding with dictators and human-rights abusers to achieve larger goals, such as forming alliances to prevent nuclear proliferation or to protect weaker nations from military aggressors.

The War Against Terrorism

No matter what dictates foreign policy—idealism or realism—a nonviolent solution, such as the use of diplomacy, cannot be found for some conflicts. If two sides of an international dispute have vastly different views of what the outcome should be and are pursuing opposing goals or views of what the world should become, it may be impossible to find a solution in which both sides get something they want. For example, during World War II, the Axis Powers (Germany, Japan, Italy, Hungary, Romania, and Bulgaria) and the Allies (the United States, England, France, the Soviet Union, Belgium, Australia, and several other countries) were fighting for completely different goals and visions of the future. The result of this disagreement was a six-year war—the most brutal in the history of the world—that killed tens of millions of people.

Today, extremists who have perverted the teachings of Islam are obsessed with pursuing a jihad—a holy war against heretics and infidels (unbelievers). Because of ideological differences and the extremity of their beliefs, their demands cannot be met by the rest of the world. For instance, terrorist groups such as al-Qaeda, which frequently attack civilians of every faith around the world, have declared that the only concession they want from infidels is for them to die.

Americans have been the victims of such attacks on several occasions, as when a Marine barracks in Beirut was bombed on October 23, 1983, during the Lebanese civil war, killing 241 American soldiers. The first such attack to occur on American soil was in 1993, when members of the al-Qaeda terrorist group allegedly planted a bomb in the underground parking garage of the World Trade Center in New York City, killing six people and injuring scores more. The second attack on an American target occurred when al-Qaeda terrorists hijacked four commercial airlines, flew two into the World Trade Center towers in New

The Cold War

The Cold War, which took place between 1947 and 1991, was a period during which the United States and the Soviet Union were framed as adversaries because each was seeking to spread its own political ideology—democracy and communism, respectively—around the world. The United States' goal was to prevent the dissemination of communism in countries such as Vietnam, and US propaganda during this period framed the conflict as a battle between good and evil, between God-fearing democrats and godless communists. "The resulting anti-communist crusade was to have profound consequences for Christian America, contributing to both religious revival and religious repression in the early Cold War period," according to the *Oxford Research Encyclopedia of Religion*.

However, this propaganda was an oversimplification of the issues at hand. George Kennan was largely responsible for the United States' foreign policy of "containment"—preventing the spread of communism—implemented during President Truman's administration. Still, Kennan didn't view the Cold War in entirely black-and-white terms. "I do not think … that every measure that is damaging to international Communism is necessarily good and every measure that is acceptable to a Communist government is necessarily bad. The world is not that simple," he wrote in an article in the *Atlantic Monthly* in 1959.

In fact, Dianne Kirby argues that framing the Cold War in such simplistic terms actually prevented the resolution of the conflict, because "good and evil" are roles that cannot be easily shed. As Kirby writes, "the image of a godless and evil enemy dictated an irreconcilable conflict that precluded the very modes of diplomacy and discourse that might have helped avoid the worst excesses, costs, and consequences of the Cold War."

Mothers' Crusade For Victory Over Communism

This piece of anticommunist propaganda was released at the height of the Cold War.

York City, and sent a third into the Pentagon building in Washington, DC, on September 11, 2001, killing about three thousand people. Passengers on the fourth plane, which was believed to be headed for the US Capitol, rose up against the hijackers, and the plane crashed into a field in Pennsylvania, killing everyone aboard. In retaliation for these attacks, American troops invaded Afghanistan.

The purpose of the invasion of Afghanistan as expressed by the George W. Bush administration was to find and capture Osama bin Laden, a wealthy al-Qaeda leader who had allegedly planned the 9/11 attacks from his base in Afghanistan, and to destroy al-Qaeda training camps located there. Another objective was to topple the Taliban, a repressive, fanatical Islamist group that supported al-Qaeda and had ruled Afghanistan since 1996. The primary goal may have also been retaliatory, but secondary goals were to free the people of Afghanistan from a repressive government and help them create a democracy.

Again, however, results were often seen in the eyes of the rest of the world as an intrusion that cost the lives of many Afghan citizens and soldiers of many nationalities and did little to permanently eliminate the Taliban and al-Qaeda or to establish a better way of life for Afghans.

When American troops invaded Iraq in 2003 as part of a mission dubbed Operation Iraqi Freedom, motives were again retaliatory, but also idealistic. The Bush administration's stated goals in dispatching American military forces were to search for weapons of mass destruction that the Iraqi regime may have manufactured and stockpiled, and to free the Iraqi people from Saddam Hussein's repressive rule. Furthermore, Bush said, his administration hoped through military action to control terrorism arising from Iraq, and to help the Iraqis establish a democratic form of government. People around the world soon realized, however, that while the United States' goals may have seemed reasonable to President Bush, the results fell far short. It was soon apparent that there were no weapons of mass destruction stockpiled in Iraq. What's more, there was no evidence of ties between Hussein and al-Qaeda, and establishing a democratic form of government proved difficult. By the time US forces withdrew in December 2011, nearly 5,000 coalition forces had died and as many as 460,000 people had died as a direct or indirect result of the conflict.

Yet the country was left unstable and facing a new threat from an extremist group that had branched off from al-Qaeda and called itself the Islamic State in Iraq and Syria (ISIS). By 2014, the violent group known for committing countless murders, bombings, and kidnappings, and for enslaving thousands, controlled more than 34,000 square miles (88,060 square kilometers) in Iraq and Syria, and more than one million Iraqis had been displaced in the fighting. Coalition forces, including the United States, began carrying out airstrikes against ISIS in aid of Iraqi forces. After three years of violence and mass displacement, the Iraqi military reclaimed the strategic city of Mosul in 2017 and by December declared it had "fully liberated" all of the country's territory from ISIS.

According to Stephen Prothero, chair of the Department of Religion at Boston University, and author of *Religious Literacy: What Every American Needs to Know About Religion—And Doesn't*, one major reason for the failure of the Bush administration to accomplish its goals in Iraq was ignorance of the country's religion. Government officials may have understood the politics, economy, and ethnicity of Iraq, Prothero told the audience at the Pew Forum Faith Angle Conference in December 2007, "But I don't think we understood it as a religious place, where religious reasons mattered, where people were, perhaps in many cases, primarily motivated by religion."

Today, many Americans express a distrust toward Muslims, much of which stems from a lack of familiarity with Islam, a peaceful religion that expressly prohibits murder, violence, and converting people by force, as groups such as ISIS have sought to do. During the 2016 presidential election, President Obama came under fire from candidate Trump for refusing to use the term "Islamic terrorism." That fall, Obama explained his reasoning:

[W]hat I have been careful about when I describe these issues is to make sure that we do not lump these murderers into the billion Muslims that exist around the world, including in this country, who are peaceful, who are responsible, who, in this country, are fellow troops and police officers and fire fighters and teachers and neighbors and friends ... If you had an organization that was going around killing and blowing people up and said, "We're on the vanguard of Christianity," as a Christian, I'm not going to let them claim my religion and say, "you're killing for Christ." I would say, that's ridiculous ... That's not what my religion stands for. Call these folks what they are, which is killers and terrorists.

Buddhism and the Vietnam War

History has reinforced the lesson that failing to recognize how religion influences foreign relations has been costly to the United States. In the early 1960s, American foreign policy under President John F. Kennedy and later under Presidents Lyndon B. Johnson and Richard M. Nixon consisted largely of attempts to contain the advancement of communism around the world. During this period, called the Cold War, the communist threat dominated US foreign relations. In line with the containment policy, in 1965 the United States sent military troops into Vietnam to prevent the collapse of the South Vietnamese government, which was under siege from communist troops in North Vietnam. The war in Vietnam was fought largely over political ideology and nationalism, but it also had a religious component.

Surveys taken in the 1960s showed that approximately 70 percent of the Vietnamese population was Buddhist. The French who had occupied Vietnam until 1954 were largely Catholic, and under their rule, 10 percent of the citizens of South Vietnam had converted to Catholicism. The French had been aware of the threat that Buddhism posed to their authority and had passed laws to limit its growth while they were in power.

On May 8, 1963, Buddhist worshippers assembled in Hue, South Vietnam, to celebrate the 2,527th birthday of the Buddha. The president of South Vietnam, Ngo Dinh Diem, was Catholic and had appointed many Catholics to positions in his government. Diem's police attempted to disperse the Buddhist celebrants by firing into the crowd, and a woman and eight children were killed as they tried to flee. The Buddhists were furious and held many public demonstrations to protest, but Diem refused to repeal any of the anti-Buddhist laws that the French had passed.

Finally, in June 1963, Thich Quang Duc, a sixty-six-year-old Buddhist monk, sat down in the middle of a busy Saigon road and voluntarily allowed Buddhist monks and nuns to douse him with gasoline, then set him on fire in protest. Witnesses said the monk did not make a sound or move a muscle while the fire raged. While Thich Quang Duc was burning to death, the monks and nuns distributed flyers that called for the government to show "charity and compassion" to all religions. Diem's response to the suicide was to arrest thousands of Buddhist monks, a number of whom were never heard from again.

By August 1963, five more Buddhist monks had set fire to themselves. One member of the South Vietnamese government responded to the suicides by telling a newspaper reporter: "Let them burn, and we shall clap our hands." International news photographers captured the suicides, and to much of the world, the United States, in its support for South Vietnam, appeared to be backing the wrong side.

The United States began withdrawing troops from Vietnam in 1973. In the end, a total of 58,000 American troops died in Vietnam and more than 300,000 were wounded. After the war, the Vietnamese government in Hanoi released the figures for civilian dead: two million in North Vietnam and two million in South Vietnam. The civilian death toll equaled approximately 12 to 13 percent of the entire population of Vietnam. Since the war ended, North and South Vietnam, which are presently united as one country, have remained under communist rule.

US Relations with Iran

When President Jimmy Carter took office in 1977, he inherited from previous administrations a friendly relationship with Mohammad Reza Shah Pahlavi, the shah of Iran. The United States had maintained a working relationship with the shah since 1953, the year the US Central Intelligence Agency (CIA) engineered a coup that ousted an elected but anti-Western Iranian prime minister and installed the shah. Once in control, the shah proved to be a ruthless dictator whose secret police were widely feared for their expertise in torture.

A little-noticed event in Iran in the 1960s was the shah's ouster of an obscure Iranian Shiite cleric, Ayatollah Ruhollah Khomeini, who protested the shah's regime. Khomeini fled to France but continued to communicate with the Iranian people via telephone and smuggled cassette tapes. While Khomeini secretly amassed loyal followers in Iran, the shah killed the cleric's son, declared martial law, and ordered his troops to shoot at a crowd of unarmed demonstrators, killing nine hundred.

The US government was alarmed at the turmoil in Iran, but Carter's administration continued to support the shah, even when he refused to adopt reforms that might restore calm. The Iranian people constantly revolted against the shah through violent public demonstrations and strikes, and when he finally left the country in 1979, Khomeini returned to seize power. He declared a new Islamic Republic, where all laws governing the country were based on the Islamic holy book, the Quran. Khomeini whipped his followers into an anti-American frenzy that some sources believe has led to an ongoing hatred in Iran of all things American.

After the shah was deposed on November 4, 1979, Iranian student militants stormed the US embassy in Tehran and captured sixty-six US diplomats and other employees stationed there. President Carter made an ill-advised attempt to rescue the hostages via helicopter, but the helicopter crashed before reaching its destination, and the rescue mission failed. The hostages were released a few at a time through 1979 and 1980, and all fifty-two remaining captives were freed on January 20, 1981. The hostage crisis lasted 444 days.

Madeleine Albright, former member of the National Security Council, US ambassador to the United Nations, and secretary of state under President Bill Clinton, wrote of that time in *The Mighty and the Almighty*:

——

We were caught off guard by the revolution in Iran for the simple reason that we had never seen anything like it. As a political force, Islam was thought to be waning, not rising. Everyone in the region was presumed to be preoccupied with the practical problems of economics and modernization. A revolution in Iran based on a religious backlash against America and the West? Other than a few fanatics, who would support such a thing?

The situation in Iran brought home to the US government in no uncertain terms that in foreign affairs, religion counts.

One reason the revolution in Iran was so shocking to American policymakers was that, up to that time, they had no preparation in terms of learning about religion in other parts of the world and no source of advice on the topic within the government. Albright wrote: "When I was secretary of state, I had an entire bureau of economic experts I could turn to, and a cadre of experts on non-proliferation and arms control whose mastery of technical jargon earned them a nickname, 'the priesthood.'" Yet Albright had no one within the government to whom she could turn for advice and instruction on combining religious principles with diplomacy. "Given the nature of today's world, knowledge of this type is essential," she added.

Religion's Role in Foreign Affairs

In 1994, as it was becoming increasingly clear that religion matters in foreign relations, the Center for Strategic and International Studies published *Religion, the Missing Dimension of Statecraft*.

About the same time the book was published, its coauthor, Douglas Johnston, a former naval officer and senior official in the US Department of Defense, founded the International Center for Religion and Diplomacy (ICRD) to study faith-based diplomacy and play a mediating role in some of the world's religious conflicts, such as those in Pakistan, Iran, and the Sudan.

Why is religion important to international relations? In a speech delivered to a US Department of State Open Forum in December 2006, Johnston explained that in nearly every current global conflict, there is a religious component, as in Iraq, Afghanistan, Lebanon, Chechnya, Kosovo, and other areas around the globe:

Whether religion is a root cause of the conflict as it probably comes closest to being in the Middle East (where there are competing religious claims for the same piece of territory), or merely a badge of identity and mobilizing vehicle for nationalist or ethnic passions (as has typically been the case in the Balkans), it is nevertheless central to much of the strife that is taking place.

The United States has had difficulty dealing effectively with religious conflicts, Johnston claims, because our diplomats approach global strife from two positions: first, rational decision-making, which views religion as irrational and therefore excludes it from the process; second, the American belief in separation of church and state, which is ingrained in American political thought and therefore carries over into international relations.

However, separating religion from government is a foreign concept to those who follow the Islamic faith, Johnston has stated.

"We say 'secular,' they hear 'Godless,' when what was intended was 'freedom to worship as you please.' They hear 'Godless' in large part because of the cultural image we project."

The ICRD trains religious scholars on all sides of a conflict who then discuss possible solutions. For example, a young woman from a village in Pakistan, near the Afghanistan and Iran borders, was caught talking on a cell phone at 2:00 a.m. to a young man she liked. This was a violation of tribal custom, and the village elders decided that, as punishment, the girl, her mother, her sister, and the boy's mother should all die. The boy would lose his nose and ears as punishment. A local religious school leader who had participated in ICRD discussions on human rights heard about the situation and respectfully asked the girl's village elders if he could mediate on the basis of principles taught in the Quran. Much to his relief, he won permission, and he first pointed out that the Quran has no restrictions on a woman talking to a man. He also read selected passages from the Quran encouraging peaceful solutions to problems and respect for others, and he was able to negotiate a solution in which no one was harmed. Johnston points out, however, that since tribal customs are three thousand years old and Islam is only fourteen hundred years old, a solution that goes against tribal customs is not always possible.

Success in foreign relations today demands that the US government and its representatives around the globe have a nuanced understanding of the religious history and tenets that underlie and inform other countries' policies and laws. Such understanding cultivates peace over war, understanding over conflict, and collaboration over confrontation.

Four-in-ten countries have official state religions or preferred religions

Among the 199 countries analyzed, a breakdown of the state's relationship with religion

Official state religion	**Preferred/favored** religion	**No official or preferred** religion	**Hostile** to religious institutions
43 countries (22%)	**40** (20%)	**106** (53%)	**10** (5%)

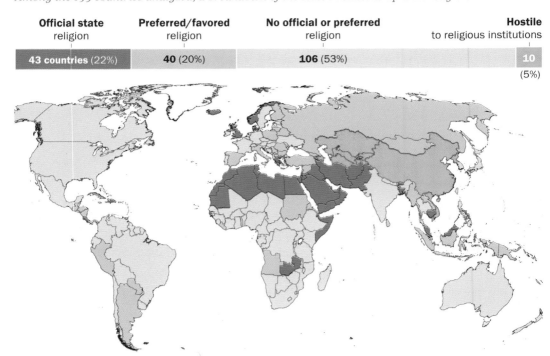

Source: Pew Research Center analysis of external data. See Methodology for details.
"Many Countries Favor Specific Religions, Officially or Unofficially"

PEW RESEARCH CENTER

Chapter Seven

GLOBAL AND US POLICIES

More than eighty countries—four in ten of all the world's countries—favor a particular religion in some way, the Pew Research Center reported in 2017. Islam was the faith most commonly endorsed by governments, with twenty-seven countries—most of them in North Africa and the Middle East—adopting it as the state religion. Thirteen countries had adopted a Christian denomination as their state religion, but forty other governments unofficially favored a specific religion, and most of these favored some branch of Christianity. Ten countries, including China, were considered hostile toward religious institutions. A total of 59 percent of people around the globe favored the separation of church and state in 2017.

Opposite: According to data published by the Pew Research Center in 2017, about 40 percent of countries have an official or preferred state religion or religions (*shown in blue and light blue*).

Just as each country varies in terms of which religion is most dominant among its population, countries also vary widely in the degree of separation between their governments and religion, and the degree to which their governments grant religious freedom. In fact, the promotion of religious freedom in countries around the world has become a core objective of the United States' foreign policy and an important mission of the US Department of State.

Religion and the State, Around the World

Most European countries have constitutions that grant religious freedom, and most protect this freedom. Some designate a state religion, which means that they may also support the state religion through public monies.

The United Kingdom (UK), which includes England, Wales, Scotland, and Northern Ireland, protects freedom of religion constitutionally and prohibits discrimination based on religion through laws that include its Employment Equality Regulations; the Anti-Terrorism, Crime, and Security Act; and the Racial and Religious Hatred Act. The UK has two established, or state, churches: the Church of England (Anglican) and the Church of Scotland (Presbyterian). However, the government has emphasized that the establishment of state churches is deeply ingrained in the nation's history but does not preclude citizens from joining other churches or practicing the religion of their choice.

France practices a more complete separation of church and state than the UK. A 1905 law on the separation of church and state prohibits discrimination on the basis of religion. The French Constitution of the Fifth Republic, adopted in 1958, declares the country to be "an indivisible, secular, democratic, and social Republic."

French citizens have a variety of constitutional rights, including the presumption of innocence, the guarantee of property ownership against arbitrary seizure, accountability of government agents to the citizens, freedom of speech, freedom of opinion, and freedom of religion. France does not designate or support a state religion, but those who practice the Jewish, Catholic, Lutheran, and Reformed religions may designate a portion of their income tax payments to go to their church. Private schools, including religious schools, are subsidized by the government.

Several French laws in the past few decades have aroused some controversy around questions of religious freedom. A government commission on sects established in 1996 designated the Jehovah's Witnesses a criminal sect because of their prohibition on blood transfusions. In 2004, the French government passed a law that banned wearing conspicuous religious symbols in public schools, which included the headscarves, called hijabs, that female Muslims typically wear, yarmulkes worn by Jews, and large crosses worn by Christians. However, the law was controversial in some circles, seen by many to specifically target Muslims. It was nonetheless upheld by the European court of human rights in 2014.

While Article 4 of Germany's Basic Law for the Federal Republic guarantees citizens freedom of faith, creed, conscience, and the practice of religion, in recent years the country has come under attack for its treatment of certain religious minorities. Three faiths—Lutheran, Catholic, and Jewish—enjoy special corporate status under the law, which allows them specific tax advantages. Church schools receive government subsidies, and public schools provide religious instruction in the three favored faiths. Minority religions may be tax-exempt, but the German government has been accused of discriminating against some minority religions.

In an example of discrimination against a religion, members of the Unification Church, founded by the Reverend Sun Myung Moon, have been banned from entering Germany as part of the nation's anticult campaign. (Bans against members of the Unification Church are also in place in other European countries for the same reason.) The church has also been denied tax-exempt status in Germany, the stated reason being that it is a "danger to the public good." Unification Church beliefs are based on Moon's book, *Divine Principle*, and include the belief in a universal God; in the creation of a Kingdom of Heaven on Earth; and in the possibility of salvation for all people, good and evil, as well as living and dead. Unification Church members are also taught that Jesus did not come to Earth for the express purpose of dying, and that the second coming of Christ was a man born in Korea in the early twentieth century—Sun Myung Moon, the man who founded the church.

Like the constitutions of most European countries, Italy's constitution provides for freedom of religion, and the government generally protects this freedom in practice. The Roman Catholic Church's longstanding association with the government has resulted in some concessions to that religion, but as of 1984, the nation's constitution had declared that the government and the Roman Catholic Church are independent and sovereign. In 1984, an agreement was signed between the government and the Vatican stating that Catholicism would no longer be Italy's state religion and that Rome would no longer retain the "sacred character of eternal city." (Vatican City, the official government ruled by the pope, is located within the city of Rome.) However, members of the Roman Catholic Church, the Assembly of God Church, and the Adventist Church may make arrangements to have a portion of their taxes donated to their respective churches.

Governmental Agencies Supporting Religious Freedom

In 1998, during Madeleine Albright's tenure as secretary of state, Congress passed the International Religious Freedom Act to

Separation of Church and State Around the World

Country	Constitution Grants Religious Freedom	State-Designated Religion	Financial Benefits and/or Tax Subsidies	Mandatory Religious Instruction in Public Schools
Norway	Yes	Yes—Evangelical Lutheranism	Yes	Yes
Greece	Yes, with some stipulations	Yes—Eastern Orthodox	Yes	Yes, for Orthodox students only
Turkey	Yes, with some restrictions	No, but most citizens are Muslim	Yes	Yes
Russia	Yes, with legal restrictions on many denominations other than Russian Orthodox	No, but Russian Orthodox is the dominant religion	Yes, for Russian Orthodox Church	Yes
India	Yes	No	Yes, legally mandated benefits are awarded to specific groups	No
China	No—religious repression existed until the 1980s; religious revival continues to the present	No. The government allows five religions to operate legally so long as they're members of "patriotic associations."	No—religious activity is highly regulated and restricted	No
Japan	Yes	No. Buddhism and Shinto are dominant; cults are regulated and restricted.	No, but registered "religious corporations" are tax-exempt	No
Iran	No—the government is a theocracy	Yes—Islam; other religions severely restricted	Yes	Yes

promote religious freedom as a goal of US international relations policy. Within the US Department of State, the act established:

- An ambassador-at-large for religious freedom.
- A Commission on International Religious Freedom.
- A bipartisan commission on international religious freedom.
- A special advisor on international religious freedom within the National Security Council.

The US Department of State's Commission on International Religious Freedom promotes freedom of religion throughout the world as an inalienable human right. According to its website, the office seeks to:

- Promote freedom of religion and conscience throughout the world as a fundamental human right and as a source of stability for all countries.
- Assist emerging democracies in implementing freedom of religion and conscience.
- Assist religious and human rights NGOs in promoting religious freedom.
- Identify and denounce regimes that are severe persecutors on the basis of religious belief.

Under the auspices of the Freedom of Religion Act, the Department of State prepares an annual International Religious Freedom Report using information provided by American embassies around the world and a variety of other sources. The report names those countries where religious freedom is denied with the intention of impeding the progress of religious persecution in those countries. The process used to prepare the report—investigating, documenting, and protesting abuses—has helped to prevent or tone down some religious persecution that would otherwise occur.

In early 2018, the countries shown in orange above had been named Countries of Particular Concern with regards to religious freedom.

As the reports are compiled, the US Department of State also prepares a list of "Countries of Particular Concern" under the International Religious Freedom Act. Those countries listed are then subject to US actions that usually include economic sanctions. The countries on the list in early 2018 included Burma, the Central African Republic, China, Eritrea, Iran, Russia, North Korea, Saudi Arabia, and Nigeria. The Department of State uses the following list of possible abuses to determine whether a country should be listed as one of particular concern:

- Totalitarian and authoritarian regimes may attempt to control religious thought and action. Such regimes regard some or all religions as enemies of the state and persecute them accordingly.
- Governments may be hostile to minority or non-state-approved religions, intimidating or harassing them.

- The state may simply fail to address either societal discrimination or societal abuses against religious groups. Legislation may discourage such abuse, but officials fail to prevent it.
- Governments pass discriminatory laws against certain minority or non-state-sanctioned religions.
- Governments discriminate against certain religions by designating them as dangerous cults or sects.

In any discussion on the status of freedom of religion around the world, it is important to remember that nonbelievers, in a country where freedom of religion is respected, have the same rights as believers. Just as Muslims, Catholics, Protestants, Jews, Buddhists, Hindus, and all believers should have the basic human right to worship when, where, and how they please, so, too, must nonbelievers have the right not to worship at all.

Pope Francis, head of the Catholic Church, has proclaimed his belief in the freedom of religion, a noteworthy affirmation from an institution that once effectively ruled the most powerful nations on earth. "We must promote religious liberty for all people. Every man and woman must be free to profess his or her faith, whatever it may be," the pope said in 2013.

Religious Freedom as a Global Right

The United Nations is also concerned with the status of religious freedom around the world. In the UN's Universal Declaration of Human Rights of 1948, citizens of every nation were proclaimed to possess certain human rights, including the right to freedom of religion. Similarly, the International Covenant on Civil and Political Rights of 1966 proclaimed the right of all people to "self-determination," which included the right to "freely determine their political status and freely pursue their economic, social, and cultural development."

The United States and the UN are concerned about religious freedom around the world because it is closely associated with all civil liberties. If freedom of speech is restricted in a country, generally religious speech is also restricted. If freedom to assemble is not allowed, it follows that assembling for worship is not allowed. Where men are viewed as religious heads of households, women's rights are generally restricted. And if a country has a state religion, failure to attend a state-sanctioned church (or any church) can result in severe penalties. It is crucial, therefore, that governments respect all human rights, so that each individual freedom is equally protected.

Furthermore, religious liberty is strongly associated with political, social, and ethnic identity, which makes it integral to one's deepest belief systems and sense of personal identity. For this reason, it is understandable that citizens want their government to reflect those morals and principles that form the core of their belief. The question remains, however—given that belief systems vary with individuals, if the government becomes involved in furthering or hindering any one religion or specific religions, who will choose the religion(s) to be favored? And will it become easy for governments, made up of individuals, to persecute those associated with religions that are not favored?

Chapter Eight

LIVING UNDER RELIGIOUS RULE

In February 2018, twenty-nine people were arrested in Iran after protesting their country's legally enforced dress code, which—among other things—requires that all women wear a traditional headscarf called a hijab. Women throughout Iran had been pictured removing their hijabs in public to protest the restrictions, and videos and photos of these defiant acts had spread across social media. Women were pictured waving their hijabs in the air like flags.

The Iranian Constitution

A legally mandated dress code is not common in countries that enforce a strict separation between

Opposite: During 2017 demonstrations, Vida Movahed takes off her state-mandated headscarf in a street in Tehran, Iran, to protest the law requiring that she wear it. She was arrested.

church and state. However, Iranians have lived under strict Islamic law (sharia law) since Iran's constitution was rewritten after the 1979 revolution to conform to the Quran. Article 4 of the Iranian constitution says: "All laws and regulations including civil, criminal, financial, economic, administrative, cultural, military, political or otherwise, shall be based on Islamic principles. This Article shall apply generally to all the Articles of the Constitution and to other laws and regulations."

After the United States–supported shah departed in 1979, Ayatollah Ruhollah Khomeini, a revered imam (Muslim religious leader), assumed power as the supreme leader of Iran. As provided in the constitution, the supreme leader is the highest official state authority (Article 113). He is chosen by the Leadership Experts or leadership Khobregan, a division of the Faqihs (jurists on religious law). All Leadership Experts must be clergymen, and they supervise the supreme leader, who is also a clergyman.

Iran's constitution also provides for the election of a president, whose duties are restricted to the implementation of the constitution. All other governmental authority falls to the supreme leader. The president is elected by direct vote of the people. The judicial branch of government and representatives of the Majlis (Islamic Consultative Assembly), who are also elected, supervise the president.

While the constitution of the Islamic Republic of Iran also calls for three branches of government—legislative, executive, and judicial—the authority of the supreme leader supersedes that of all other branches and offices of government. In fact, if the supreme leader violates the constitution using Islamic rules for justification, no one is empowered to oppose him.

Once the 1979 constitution was in place, Khomeini formally assumed his position as supreme leader. Khomeini died on June 4, 1989, at the age of eighty-seven. Tehran Radio announced the death, illustrating the reverence with which faithful Muslim

Iranians regarded the spiritual and political leader: "The lofty spirit of the leader of the Muslims and the leader of the noble ones, His Eminence Imam Khomeini, has reached the highest status, and a heart replete with love and God and his true people, who have endured numerous hardships, has stopped beating."

On the day of the deceased imam's burial, Ayatollah Khomeini's body, wrapped in a white burial shroud, was laid in an open coffin and was carried to the cemetery. Members of the crowd along the route, hysterical with grief, grabbed at the body, hoping to tear away a piece of the shroud to keep as a memento. The men holding the litter were jostled, the burial box tipped, and the Ayatollah's body fell to the ground. Revolutionary guards escorting the funeral procession beat back the crowd while the ruler's body was replaced in its burial box. A helicopter hovering overhead dropped low enough to snatch the body and carry it away from the grief-stricken mourners. Hours later, the Ayatollah reached his final resting place.

The Khomeini era, which lasted ten years, is known for redefining Iran as a republic ruled by the laws of Islam.

Today, Ayatollah Ali Khamenei is the supreme leader of the Islamic Republic of Iran. In his position as spiritual head of the government, Khamenei has designated prayer leaders in each city and representatives in each major government office that give him eyes and ears everywhere. Furthermore, he selects the members of the Guardian Council, which must approve all legislation passed by the parliament, or Majlis. He closely controls the country's radio and television networks, whose director he appoints. He appoints the heads of the clerical court and the regular judiciary, who in turn appoint the nation's other judges. He is also head of the seminary system (*rais-e howzeh*).

What's more, Khamenei controls the key instruments of national security: the Islamic Revolutionary Guard Corps (IRGC), the politically active Basij paramilitary, and the KGB-

Expression and Social Interaction in Iran

In today's Iran, under the written word of the Quran, five themes are reinforced by law:

- The call to worship
- The need for justice
- The worthlessness of paganism
- The inevitability of the Day of Judgment and the punishments for evildoers
- The reward of paradise for the faithful

Under these mandates, Islamic law calls for the government's enforcement of public morality. Iranian moral offenses, for which the police can arrest violators, include:

- Terrorizing others by quarreling and feuding in public
- Women failing to cover up in a suitable way:
  - Legs must not be exposed
  - Hats must not be substituted for scarves, which must cover the hair
  - High-heeled shoes and sandals are not acceptable
  - Designer handbags are forbidden
  - Bejeweled sunglasses are prohibited
  - Makeup is forbidden
- Either sex wearing decadent Western clothing
- Viewing decadent films
- Drinking alcohol or taking drugs
- General thuggish behavior
- Displaying signs and insignia of deviant groups

In a bazaar in Tehran, Iran, women are pictured in state-approved garb as they do their shopping.

Other offenses that can lead to arrest include unmarried couples walking hand-in-hand or sitting together on park benches, a man holding a woman's waist while walking in a shopping complex, a woman leaning on a man's shoulder, sitting on a bench in the dark in a park or by a lake, and females being in places that serve alcohol. Police may seize young men with improper hair lengths and forcibly cut their hair.

Iranian stores that sell clothing are also subject to government regulations, and in one recent crackdown, store managers were ordered to cut the breasts off of realistically constructed female mannequins. Some shops are sealed, and others are warned not to sell tight, revealing clothing.

These offenses are punishable by jail terms, fines, and caning, depending upon the seriousness of the offense and the behavior of the offender at the time of arrest. Other, more serious morality offenses, such as homosexuality and women who commit adultery (men are seldom punished as adulterers, and can take more than one wife), can be punished by torture and death.

like Ministry of Intelligence and Security (charged with security operations both at home and abroad). Nuclear negotiations with the West are conducted by Khamenei's representative with little or no input from the Ministry of Foreign Affairs.

Iran's president, Hassan Rouhani, promised to improve civil rights when he was elected in 2013, and was generally seen as a moderate in comparison to his predecessor, Mahmoud Ahmadinejad. However, by late 2017 and early 2018, the Iranian economy was sluggish, most of the promised reforms had not been implemented, and protests broke out throughout the country.

From an economic standpoint, oil and natural gas earn approximately $1,300 per year for each Iranian. Iran's central bank prints currency, which has pushed inflation up to about 25 percent per year, and unemployment remains above 11 percent. Rural Iranians support Islamists because they have been promised government support. Modernists look to the West for inspiration, and many have left Iran to live in other countries where freedom of religion and freedom of expression exist. In a country where Islam regulates every facet of existence, many cannot imagine their lives outside of Muslim traditionalism. Islamic Iran promises protection to its subjects against a threatening outside world, and apparently hopes to force other countries to submit to Islamic standards—if only through the threat of nuclear proliferation.

Saudi Arabia

As in Iran, Islamic law controls life for residents of Saudi Arabia. Women—both citizens and visitors—are expected to wear appropriate dress, which means arms, legs, and hair are covered. Muslim Saudi women generally wear the traditional abaya, which is a shapeless black, gray, dark blue, or white floor-length garment that covers the entire body, including the arms. Muslim women also wear a scarf that completely covers their hair, and they may also wear a veil to cover their faces. Failure to dress appropriately can result in arrest for Saudi women.

Saudi Arabia's version of sharia law has forbidden women to drive or drink alcohol, and also forbids any citizen to practice Western vices. (In September 2017, the government announced it would allow women to drive beginning in June 2018.) Cigarettes are allowed, but no public movie theaters, public bowling alleys, bars or nightclubs, and no churches—mosques are the only worship centers that receive government approval. All restaurants have two sections—a section for single males and a family section. Women dining as a group with female friends must sit in the family section or risk arrest for prostitution.

As in Iran, Islamic law mandates prayer five times a day for Muslims in Saudi Arabia. In most Middle Eastern countries where Islam is dominant, businesses allow prayer breaks for the faithful but do not close. In Saudi Arabia, however, stores and restaurants close during prayer times. If shoppers or diners happen to be inside a business when prayer time is called, they are locked in but can continue to eat or shop. Lights are dimmed, however, so after-dark diners sometimes carry candles if the meal will extend through the mid-evening prayer call.

Afghanistan

Afghanistan under Taliban rule was perhaps the strictest of those countries where Islamic law presides. Before the United States and Great Britain invaded Afghanistan in October 2001, the radical group called the Taliban controlled approximately 95 percent of the country, including the capital of Kabul and most of the largest urban areas. (The invasion was in retaliation for the September 11, 2001, attacks on the World Trade Center and the Pentagon, which were planned by Osama bin Laden, an al-Qaeda leader living in Afghanistan with the Taliban's blessing.)

The pre-invasion Afghanistan government was a brutal, repressive theocracy. A Taliban edict in 1997 renamed the country the Islamic Emirate of Afghanistan, with Taliban leader Mullah (a title of respect for a Muslim cleric) Omar as Head of State and Commander of the Faithful. There was a six-member ruling council in Kabul, but ultimate authority for Taliban rule rested in Mullah Omar, head of the inner Shura (council), located in the southern city of Kandahar. There was no recognized constitution, rule of law, or independent judiciary that applied countrywide, and the Taliban was Afghanistan's primary military force and law-enforcement body. In 2000, the country was the largest opium producer in the world.

Women in Afghanistan were especially oppressed. In fact, under the Taliban, Afghan women suffered a complete loss of human rights. After the Taliban assumed power in 1996, women were required to wear the burka in public, a shapeless garment that covered the entire body. Headscarves and veils were also

Taliban rebels sought to impose their strict version of Islamic law on Afghanistan during the 1990s.

mandatory, and the veils had to cover the entire face—including the eyes. Women were severely beaten or stoned for appearing in public with any part of their bodies showing.

Women were not allowed to work or to appear in public without a male relative. To appear in public with a man who was not a relative was justification for a woman to receive a public lashing. Married women accused of adultery could be stoned to death. Professional women, including professors, doctors, lawyers, teachers, engineers, artists, and writers, who had careers before the Taliban assumed power, were forced to leave their jobs to keep house for their husbands. Households where a woman was present were to have the windows painted over, and women were told to wear soft shoes so that men would not hear them when they walked. If a woman had no man for financial support, she was forced to beg in the streets or starve to death.

Women under Taliban rule were not allowed to attend school (girls' schools were converted to religious seminaries for males only), and there were no medical facilities for women. Husbands had complete control over the lives of female relatives—especially wives—and women lived in constant fear for their lives.

Requirements for men—wearing a turban, allowing facial hair to grow, and observing all additional Islamic rules—seemed tame by comparison to those restrictions imposed on women.

The 2001 United States–United Kingdom invasion of Afghanistan toppled the Taliban, but because of a reduction in the occupying military forces, the Taliban has since regained some control. As of late 2017, coinciding with the drawdown of US troops in Afghanistan, the Taliban were mounting suicide bombings throughout the country. However, in a January 2018 article in *Foreign Affairs*, Seth G. Jones—director of the Transnational Threats Program at the Center for Strategic and International and former senior advisor to the Commanding

General of US Special Operations in Afghanistan—argued that the Taliban doesn't have popular support:

———

> [The Taliban's] ideology is still too extreme for many Afghans—including urban Afghans—who adhere to a much less conservative form of Islam that permits most modern technology, music, political participation, and some rights for women. For example, nearly all Afghans say they approve of women voting, while girls, barred from education under the Taliban, now account for 39 percent of public school students in Afghanistan. The Afghan Parliament has set aside 69 of the 249 seats in its lower house for women, while the upper house includes 27 female members of parliament out of its 102 members.

In a 2015 poll, only 4 percent of Afghans favored the Taliban.

A Delicate Balance

When existing theocracies are examined and compared with those countries that practice separation of church and state, many people believe that while freedom of religion must be constitutionally defined and legally maintained, governments best serve citizens and best protect their human rights when they neither embrace nor reject religion.

Clyde Wilcox and Carin Larson, authors of *Onward Christian Soldiers?: The Religious Right in American Politics*, remind those on both sides of the separation of church and state debate that because the issue has become divided along political lines, "there has been more shouting than discussion, and both sides have ended up

adopting more extreme positions in an effort to mobilize voters. Between the shouting voices there is room for a quieter discussion, where both sides might be surprised that they have some common ground."

Understanding the debate from all sides can lead to surprising revelations like this. After all, six in ten people in the world believe that a separation of church and state is valuable, and that the freedoms it promotes are worthwhile and necessary. But achieving this separation requires a delicate balance, one in which religions are respected but not promoted or mandated, in which laws reflect moral and ethical principles without depriving anyone of their rights. The debate on how to strike this balance continues, each side speaking its mind—the very act of debate a freedom in itself.

In 2015, Danish people of Christian, Muslim, and Jewish faiths surround a Copenhagen synagogue to symbolize peace after a Jewish security guard was shot there earlier that year.

agnostic Someone who neither believes nor disbelieves in the existence of God.

apostate One who commits apostasy—that is, who refuses to recognize or obey a religious faith.

atheist A person who does not believe in the existence of a god or gods.

Bible The sacred book in Christianity; consists of the sixty-six books of the Old and New Testaments.

creationism A doctrine holding that God created life out of nothing, usually in the way described in Genesis.

crèche In this case, a model showing the scene of Jesus Christ's birth, often put on display during Christmas season.

drawdown A reduction in the size or presence of a military force.

evolution A scientific theory explaining the appearance of new species and varieties through various biological mechanisms, including natural selection and hybridization, involving descent with modification over time.

extremist A person who advocates extreme or radical measures or views.

hijab A traditional covering for the hair and neck worn by Muslim women.

homosexuality Sexual attraction or the tendency to direct sexual desire toward another of the same sex.

imam The prayer leader of a mosque.

magistrate An official entrusted with the administration of laws, such as a local administrator or judge.

parochial Of or relating to a church parish, or to religion more generally.

Quran The sacred book in Islam; believed to be God's word as dictated to the prophet Muhammad.

secular Of or relating to the worldly or temporal; not religious.

sedition Incitement of resistance to or insurrection against lawful authority.

shah A sovereign of Iran.

temperance Moderation in or abstinence from the consumption of alcohol.

Torah The sacred book in Judaism; believed to be the law of God as revealed to Moses.

transubstantiation The miraculous change by which, in Roman Catholic and Eastern Orthodox dogma, bread and wine at their consecration become the body and blood of Christ.

Further Information

Books

Cahill, Bryon. *Freedom to Worship*. South Egremont, MA: Red Chair Press, 2014.

Green, Steven K. *Inventing a Christian America: The Myth of the Religious Founding*. Oxford, UK: Oxford University Press, 2015.

Lambert, Frank. *Separation of Church and State: Founding Principle of Religious Liberty*. Macon, GA: Mercer University Press, 2014.

Porterfield, James. *The Separation of Church and State: Interpreting the Constitution*. New York: Rosen Young Adult, 2014.

Websites

Cornell Law School Legal Information Institute: First Amendment
http://www.law.cornell.edu/constitution/first_amendment
This site offers a wealth of resources on the First Amendment to the Constitution and its clauses pertaining to freedom of religion.

God in America
http://www.pbs.org/godinamerica/view
This documentary tells the story of the four-hundred-year debate about religion in public life in the United States.

Scopes Trial
http://www.pbs.org/wgbh/evolution/library/08/2/l_082_01.html

This site includes information on the famous Scopes trial of 1925 and a video accompaniment.

Videos

JFK: Church and State
https://www.youtube.com/watch?v=iDP4qrA8hvg

This video shows a speech delivered by future US president John F. Kennedy on September 12, 1960, in which he addresses concerns about his Catholic faith and asserts the importance of the separation of church and state.

The Lord Is Not on Trial Here Today
http://www.pbs.org/programs/lord-is-not-on-trial-here-today/

This PBS documentary investigates how separation of church and state came to apply in public schools.

SCOTUS to Hear Dispute Over Separation of Church and State
https://www.nbcnews.com/nightly-news/video/scotus-to-hear-dispute-over-separation-of-church-and-state-922473027673.

This video offers an overview of the separation of church and state issue involved in the Trinity Lutheran v. Comer case.

Organizations

American Civil Liberties Union
125 Broad Street, 18th Floor
New York, NY 10004
(212) 549-2500
http://www.aclu.org

The ACLU seeks to defend those rights and freedoms outlined in the US Constitution and in US legislation.

Americans United for Separation of Church and State

1310 L Street NW, Suite 200

Washington, DC 20005

(202) 466-3234

http://www.au.org

This organization of lobbyists, lawyers, activists, religious leaders, and more aims to protect the "wall" between church and state.

International Association for Religious Freedom

Essex Hall

1-6 Essex Street

London WC2R 3HY

United Kingdom

http://www.iarf.net

The IARF is the world's oldest global inter-religious organization, designed to promote interfaith dialogue and tolerance.

United States Commission on International Religious Freedom

732 North Capitol Street, NW

Suite A714

Washington, DC 20401

(202) 523-3240

http://www.uscirg.gov

The USCIRF is a US federal government commission established in 1998 with the goal of defending religious freedom outside of the United States. Here, you'll find the latest data on religious freedom in countries around the globe.

Bibliography

Albright, Madeleine. *The Mighty and the Almighty: Reflections on America, God, and World Affairs.* New York: HarperCollins Publishers, 2006.

"Arguments in Favour of Abortion." BBC, 2014. http://www.bbc.co.uk/ethics/abortion/mother/for_1.shtml.

Astor, Maggie. "Violence Against Transgender People Is on the Rise, Advocates Say." *New York Times*, November 9, 2017. https://www.nytimes.com/2017/11/09/us/transgender-women-killed.html.

Augstums, Ieva M. "Huckabee Declines Theology Discussion." *Washington Post*, December 7, 2007. http://www.washingtonpost.com/wp-dyn/content/article/2007/12/07/AR2007120700942.html.

"Benjamin Franklin on Religion." World Policy Institute. Accessed April 4, 2018. https://worldpolicy.org/wp-content/uploads/2010/04/Franklin-religion.pdf.

Beran, Stephanie. "Native Americans in Prison: The Struggle for Religious Freedom." *Nebraska Anthropologist* 2 (2005). https://digitalcommons.unl.edu/cgi/viewcontent.cgi?article=1001&context=nebanthro.

Borden, Morton. "The Christian Amendment," *Civil War History* 25, no. 2 (1979). https://muse.jhu.edu/article/419814/pdf.

Bowker, John. *Cambridge Illustrated History: Religions*. New York: Cambridge University Press, 2002.

Bush, George. "Executive Order: Establishment of White House Office of Faith-Based and Community Initiatives." White House Office of the Press Secretary, January 2001. https://georgewbush-whitehouse.archives.gov/news/releases/2001/01/20010129-2.html.

Carter, Stephen L. *God's Name in Vain: The Wrongs and Rights of Religion in Politics*. New York: Basic Books, 2000.

———. *The Culture of Disbelief: How American Law and Politics Trivialize Religious Devotion*. New York: Random House, 1993.

CNN Library. "ISIS Fast Facts." CNN, December 12, 2017. https://www.cnn.com/2014/08/08/world/isis-fast-facts/index.html.

———. "Same-Sex Marriage Fast Facts." CNN, September 7, 2017. https://www.cnn.com/2013/05/28/us/same-sex-marriage-fast-facts/index.html.

Cooper, Helene. "Transgender People Will Be Allowed to Enlist in the Military as a Court Case Advances." *New York Times*, December 11, 2017. https://www.nytimes.com/2017/12/11/us/politics/transgender-military-pentagon.html?rref=collection%2Ftimestopic%2FTransgender%20and%20Transsexuals&action=click&contentCollection=timestopics&region=stream&module=stream_unit&version=latest&contentPlacement=14&pgtype=collection.

Davis, Edwin S. "The Religion of George Washington." *Air and Space Power Journal*, July/August 1976. http://www.airuniversity. af.mil/Portals/10/ASPJ/journals/1976_Vol27_No1-6/1976_ Vol27_No5.pdf.

Diaz, Daniella. "Obama: Why I Won't Say 'Islamic Terrorism.'" CNN, September 29, 2016. https://www.cnn.com/2016/09/28/ politics/obama-radical-islamic-terrorism-cnn-town-hall/index. html.

Dreisbach, Daniel L. *Thomas Jefferson and the Wall of Separation Between Church and State*. New York: New York University Press, 2002.

Dwyer, Devin. "Faith-Based Debate: Obama Signs Order on Funds for Churches." ABC News, November 18, 2010. http://abcnews. go.com/Politics/president-obama-executive-order-faith-based- initiative-church/story?id=12180146.

Editorial Board. "The Supreme Court Weighs the Church-State Division." *New York Times Sunday Review*, April 22, 2017. https://www.nytimes.com/2017/04/22/opinion/sunday/the- supreme-court-weighs-the-church-state-division.html.

"Embryonic Stem Cell Research." Association of American Medical Colleges, 2018. https://www.aamc.org/advocacy/ research/74440/embryonicstemcellresearch.html.

"Evangelicals Rally to Trump, Religious 'Nones' Back Clinton." Pew Research Center, July 13, 2016. http://www.pewforum. org/2016/07/13/evangelicals-rally-to-trump-religious-nones- back-clinton.

"Examples of Court Decisions Supporting Coverage of LGBT-Related Discrimination Under Title VII." US Equal Employment Opportunity Commission. Accessed February 18, 2018. https://www.eeoc.gov/eeoc/newsroom/wysk/lgbt_examples_decisions.cfm.

"Faith on the Hill: The Religious Composition of the 115th Congress." Pew Research Center, January 3, 2017. http://www.pewforum.org/2017/01/03/faith-on-the-hill-115.

Feldman, Stephen M. *Please Don't Wish Me a Merry Christmas: A Critical History of the Separation of Church and State.* New York: New York University Press, 1997.

Green, Emma. "How Much Discrimination Do Muslims Face in America?" *Atlantic*, July 26, 2017. https://www.theatlantic.com/politics/archive/2017/07/american-muslims-trump/534879.

———. "The Supreme Court Strikes Down a Major Church-State Barrier." *Atlantic*, June 26, 2017. https://www.theatlantic.com/politics/archive/2017/06/trinity-lutheran/531399.

Green, Erica L. "Betsy DeVos Allies See New Obstacle to School Choice Efforts: Trump." *New York Times*, December 2, 2017. https://www.nytimes.com/2017/12/02/us/politics/betsy-devos-school-choice-vouchers-trump.html.

Hamburger, Philip. *Separation of Church and State.* Cambridge, MA: Harvard University Press, 2002.

Harrison, Frances. "'Mass Purges' at Iran Universities." BBC News, December 20, 2006. http://news.bbc.co.uk/2/hi/middle_east/6196069.stm.

"International Covenant on Civil and Political Rights." Office of the United Nations High Commissioner for Human Rights, March 23, 1976. http://www.ohchr.org/en/professionalinterest/pages/ccpr.aspx.

"James Earl Ray, Convicted King Assassin, Dies." CNN, April 23, 1998. http://www.cnn.com/US/9804/23/ray.obit.

Jefferson, Thomas. "Declaration of Independence, June 1776." National Archives. Accessed April 7, 2018. https://www.archives.gov/founding-docs/declaration-transcript.

Johnston, Douglas M. "Faith Based Diplomacy: Bridging the Religious Divide." US Department of State. Accessed April 4, 2018. https://2001-2009.state.gov/s/p/of/proc/79221.htm

Kinzer, Stephen. *Overthrow: America's Century of Regime Change from Hawaii to Iraq.* New York: Henry Holt, 2006.

Kirby, Dianne. "The Cold War and American Religion." *Oxford Research Encyclopedia of Religion*, May 2017. http://religion.oxfordre.com/view/10.1093/acrefore/9780199340378.001.0001/acrefore-9780199340378-e-398.

Kralik, Joellen. "'Bathroom Bill' Legislative Tracking." National Conference of State Legislatures, July 28, 2017. http://

www.ncsl.org/research/education/-bathroom-bill-legislative-tracking635951130.aspx.

Mackey, Sandra. *The Iranians: Persia, Islam and the Soul of a Nation*. New York: Dutton Press, 1996.

Mackintosh, Eliza. "Iranian Police Arrest 29 for Involvement in Hijab Protests." CNN, February 3, 2018. https://www.cnn.com/2018/02/02/middleeast/iran-arrests-29-women-after-hijab-protest-intl/index.html.

"Many Countries Favor Specific Religions, Officially or Unofficially." Pew Research Center, October 3, 2017. http://www.pewforum.org/2017/10/03/many-countries-favor-specific-religions-officially-or-unofficially.

McMaster, Joe. "Defending Intelligent Design." PBS, April 6, 2007. http://www.pbs.org/wgbh/nova/id/defense-id.html

Meacham, Jon. "A New American Holy War." *Newsweek*, December 17, 2007. http://www.newsweek.com/meacham-new-american-holy-war-94767.

Miller, Lisa. "Moderates Storm the Religious Battlefield." *Newsweek*, December 31, 2007–Jan. 7, 2008. http://www.newsweek.com/moderates-storm-religious-battlefield-94949.

Office of the Federal Register, National Archives and Records Administration. "Federal Register: Monday, February 9, 2009, Part IV." US Government Publishing Office, February 9, 2009. https://www.gpo.gov/fdsys/pkg/FR-2009-02-09/pdf/E9-2893.pdf.

"Pope Francis & Religious Freedom." United States Conference of Catholic Bishops, 2017. http://www.usccb.org/issues-and-action/religious-liberty/fortnight-for-freedom/upload/Pope-Francis-Quotes-on-Religious-Freedom.pdf.

"Public Makes Distinctions on Genetic Research." Pew Research Center for the People & the Press, April 9, 2002. http://peoplepress.org/reports/display.php3?ReportID=152.

Rawls, John. *Political Liberalism*. New York: Columbia University Press, 2005.

Reilly, Katie. "The Biggest Controversies from Betsy DeVos' First Year." *TIME*, December 14, 2017. http://time.com/5053007/betsy-devos-education-secretary-2017-controversies.

"Religious Freedom." US Department of State. Accessed February 18, 2018. https://www.state.gov/j/drl/irf.

"Religious Literacy: What Every American Should Know." Pew Forum Faith Angle Conference, December 3, 2007. http://pewforum.org/events/?EventID=162.

"Roe v. Wade." Planned Parenthood, 2018. https://www.plannedparenthoodaction.org/issues/abortion/roe-v-wade.

Slevin, Peter. "Kansas Education Board First to Back 'Intelligent Design.'" *Washington Post*, November 9, 2005. http://www.washingtonpost.com/wp-dyn/content/article/2005/11/08/AR2005110801211_pf.html.

Stark, Lisa. "Are School Vouchers Good for Education? That Debate Is Playing Out in Indiana." PBS NewsHour, March 14, 2017. https://www.pbs.org/newshour/show/school-vouchers-good-education-debate-playing-indiana.

"Support for Same-Sex Marriage Grows, Even Among Groups That Had Been Skeptical." Pew Research Center, June 26, 2017. http://www.people-press.org/2017/06/26/support-for-same-sex-marriage-grows-even-among-groups-that-had-been-skeptical.

"The Republicans' First Presidential Candidates Debate." *New York Times*, May 3, 2007. http://www.nytimes.com/2007/05/03/us/politics/04transcript.html.

"Tier 1 Countries of Particular Concern." United States Commission on International Religious Freedom. Accessed February 18, 2018. http://www.uscirf.gov/all-countries/countries-of-particular-concern-tier-1.

"20-Week Bans." *Rewire* Legislative Tracker, January 22, 2018. https://rewire.news/legislative-tracker/law-topic/20-week-bans.

"Washington's Farewell Address, 1796." Yale Law School, Avalon Project. Accessed April 4, 2018. http://avalon.law.yale.edu/18th_century/washing.asp.

Wilcox, Clyde, and Carin Larson. *Onward Christian Soldiers? The Religious Right in American Politics*. Cambridge, MA: Westview Press, 2006.

Willingham, A. J. "How to Make Sense of the School Choice Debate." CNN, May 24, 2017. https://www.cnn.com/2017/05/24/us/school-choice-debate-betsy-devos/index.html.

"World Religion Piechart." Adherents.com, 2005. http://www.adherents.com/Religions_By_Adherents.html.

Zauzmer, Julie. "Clergy Gather to Bless One of the Only U.S. Clinics Performing Late-Term Abortions." *Washington Post*, January 29, 2018. https://www.washingtonpost.com/news/acts-of-faith/wp/2018/01/29/clergy-gather-to-bless-an-abortion-clinic-which-provides-rare-late-term-abortions-in-bethesda/?utm_term=.8a039ecff8d9.

———. "The Complicated History of 'In God We Trust' and Other Examples Trump Gives of American Religion." *Washington Post*, February 8, 2018. https://www.washingtonpost.com/news/acts-of-faith/wp/2018/02/08/the-complicated-history-of-in-god-we-trust-and-other-examples-trump-gives-of-american-religion/?utm_term=.01a444d11036.

Index

About the Authors

Karen Judson is a former college biology instructor and has also taught high school science, kindergarten, and grades one and three. She has written about twenty books for young-adult readers, including *Animal Testing* and *Chemical and Biological Warfare*, both in Cavendish Square's Open for Debate series. In her spare time she jogs, paints wildlife scenes, and designs quilts.

Erin L. McCoy is a literature, language, and cultural studies educator and an award-winning photojournalist and poet. She holds a master of arts degree in Hispanic studies and an master of fine arts degree in creative writing from the University of Washington. She has edited nearly twenty nonfiction books for young adults, including *The Mexican-American War* and *The Israel-Palestine Border Conflict*, both part of the Redrawing the Map series with Cavendish Square Publishing. She is from Louisville, Kentucky.